EXT

TIME

EXTRA TIME

The Real Life Exploits of a Supporting Artist

John R. Walker

With Stephen Hatcher

First Published in 2012 by LULU.com

Copyright 2012 John R.Walker

ISBN 978-1-291-26400-5

Photographs Copyright 2012 John R.Walker

Cover Design ; Andrew- Mark Thompson

Typesetting ; Jason Dearn

For Robbie and Bun;

Jolly well missing you Both!

Thank you

I simply can't start this book without first of all saying,

Thank you to all the bookers who actually took the time

to telephone me and book me on these jobs. Thanks for

looking after me (and the 1000's of others)

Thanks also to my friends who are so polite when I bore

them with my on set stories, to Steve Hatcher and the

Whoovers (sounds like a band), to Jason Thomas and to

Jason Dearn who has seriously helped me out in my

hour of need. Mr. Dearn is (like Doctor Who) a fan of the

Fish Finger, so much so that he's even written the Fish

finger Sandwich book! (Order it now..), to Andrew –Mark

Thompson, Lee, Ben and to Neilum plus anyone else I

may have forgotten to mention.

Preface

You know, I cannot for the life of me, remember when I first met John, however, it would certainly have been at a meeting of the "Whoovers" Doctor Who Group in Derby, sometime in the early 2000s. It was one of those things where a stranger becomes a familiar face and then you discover that all your other friends know exactly who this person is, and he soon becomes a good friend. John became just that, as well as a lively contributor to our group's monthly meetings, long before I (at least) discovered that he did 'extra' work.

Inevitably, John's stories from the sets of Doctor Who, Torchwood, Life on Mars and so many of our favorite shows became legendary among our group members, so interviewing him on stage at our Whooverville 2 convention in September 2010 was the obvious thing to do. John was the surprise hit of the day. As respected TV historian Andrew Pixley put it, "*John Walker was also a terrific speaker; honest and modest ... and extremely good at communicating the immensely varied life of being a supporting artiste. Well worth catching John's observations about his work on 'Doctor Who', 'Torchwood' and all these other shows if you get a chance.*" (http://gallifreybase.com/forum/)

I was delighted to hear that John was writing this book, even more so when he asked me to read the first draft of Part One – and it didn't take me long to decide that not only did I want to read the whole thing, but that I also wanted to be involved in it. Thanks John for allowing me to stick my oar in!

It needs to be made clear that this is entirely 100% John's own story, mostly in his own words. My contribution has been limited to tidying up a little and making sure that John's meaning comes over clearly. If you are not happy with the content, if the book fails to engage or entertain, then blame John. If on the other hand it reads badly, if the prose is ungrammatical or inelegant, then that is my fault. As far as I can remember, the only serious disagreement we had, was over John's use of the archaic 'mobile telephone' rather than my suggested alternative 'mobile phone'. I think I won, but I look forward to finding out.

Enough from me anyway! Read the book, you'll enjoy it!

Steve Hatcher

Chapter One

It begins

Hello let me start by thanking you for buying this book and by assuring you that this is not in any way an autobiography. After all, you are hardly likely to have bought such a book written by someone whom you've never heard of. Well, let's put that right straight away, my name is John R. Walker and I am an extra! I am one of those un-credited and uncelebrated people who populate the background in TV shows and films, almost un-noticed, but adding reality and colour as you watch the stars do their thing in the foreground. What I've tried to do here is to put together my memories of working on some of my favourite TV shows of the past few years; shows such as Life on Mars and its brilliant sequel Ashes to Ashes, the revived Survivors, Being Human, Torchwood and above all, Doctor Who.

I also want to stress that I love doing extra work. I love being on set, watching shows being made from right there in the scene and being part of something so big and exciting, even if I come across as negative at any time in this book. Please believe me when I tell you how much I love it. Why else would I put this little book together and why else am I still doing extra work?

A friend of mine phoned me a few days ago and told me that he'd got a few days work in an office. I was so excited for him. It must be fantastic having a real job.

"What have you been up to this week?" he asked.

"Oh, nothing much" I replied. "On Sunday I got to push Dominic West around in a new period drama, I've been doubling for an assassin on the new Sherlock Holmes film and I am spending the rest of the week on Holby City. So, nothing much then"

I wasn't showing off, for me, that's the sort of thing I do week in and week out. After a while, it becomes pretty much run of the mill.

It was that friend who suggested that I write this book.

Despite what I said about this not being an autobiography, I think I will need to give you a very brief outline of my life, in order to give you some idea of how it was that I have come to do be involved in this peculiar line of work.

I was born in 1972 and brought up in the South West of England in the now extinct county of Avon, in a little town called Westfield-in-Radstock. As a child I wanted to be either a stunt man or a film director, but for a child living in the back of beyond, that never seemed possible. In 1987, when I was 15 years old, a friend invited me to a Doctor Who convention in Bath. I loved it! How fabulous it would be, one day, to direct a show like Doctor Who, but again that didn't seem possible.

So it was at sixteen years old, with my ambitions on hold, that I started work as a Supermarket Hygiene Technician, a.k.a. a member of the Safeway Sh1t Squad. This was just as the name suggests. My co-worker Alan and I had to clean the store. One day it could be the bakery, the next maybe the aisle floors with what looked like a toothbrush, sometime the stairs. It was a tough job but at least it was warmer than the job I'd had at a local farm sorting through potatoes.

I was at school one day when I overheard a girl tell her friend that she had applied for a job on the delicatessen counter at the Safeway supermarket in the local metropolis, Midsomer Norton. "That sounds fun", I thought, so I applied for the very same job and got it. Of course, this was only going to be a temporary arrangement, until I became a real film director!

I saved and saved and bought myself a Canon MB10 video camera, the full size one with VHS cassettes, which cost somewhere around the £1400 mark and weighed about a ton! Video cameras weren't that common back then so it provided me with a little extra income. For £50 I would video weddings and parties at the weekends. I would just dress up, turn up, shoot the hell out of the occasion and then simply give the clients the tape at the end of the night, straight out of the camera.

In 1989 Doctor Who was cancelled, just as it had started to become so amazing again. We knew it would be back. Please come back! Earlier the same year I had seen the wonderful Jon Pertwee playing the Doctor again, live on stage in Bristol in The Ultimate Adventure. In the theatre I had got chatting to the chap sitting behind me (23 years later we're still chatting). It turned out that he too had ambitions to direct and had actually already made a short film, a sequel to the 1970's classic masterpiece "Snowbeast", called "Snowbeast 2 - The Revenge of Gar". He sent me a copy and I loved it. I simply had to make the follow-up, "Snowbeast 3 - The Revenge of Gar Again"

I had no idea about framing, acting, iris control, editing, or anything camera related but this didn't stop me, I had the film bug. Over the next few years, I made a number of 'classic' films, including "Subway 2" (a sequel to the Luc Besson classic) Capricorn 2 (sequel to Capricorn One) plus "Highlander

3,4,5,6 and 7" (thankfully now lost for ever). In time we moved away from ripping off the movies and began to come up with some ideas of our own. I was film mad and most of my wages were spent on VHS tapes of every horror or science fiction film or TV show that I could get my hands on. Well I knew VHS was the way of the future!

I stayed at Safeway, accidentally becoming the youngest delicatessen manager in the company at the time, and finally moved out from my parents' house to a flat in Frome. I would spend the week running the counter and then the weekends making these awful but fun science fiction and horror films with my friends.

I discovered that Michelle, one of the check-out girls at work also wanted to get into TV. We had something in common and got on really well but then one day she told me that she was leaving work to go and do a Media Studies course in Falmouth. She will return to this story later.

In 1997 whilst reading "SFX" magazine I saw an article about a Doctor Who spin-off video called "Auton 2". I had seen the first Auton film, directed by Nicholas Briggs and produced by Bill Baggs, who had earned quite a reputation for making good quality, unofficial Doctor Who spin-off films, released straight to VHS. Baggs had acquired the rights to use a number of Doctor Who aliens, from the various original writers, who owned the rights to the names, but not the visual concepts – which belonged to the BBC. By making slight changes to how the creatures looked, he was able to avoid the wrath of the Corporation and their copyright lawyers. Anyway, the article said that Nicholas Briggs was looking for "extras" to be in the new Auton film. There was no pay, no food and no petrol allowance! What was I waiting for? I applied straight away and wrote a brilliant letter making out I knew what I was doing and that I had done this sort of thing lots of times.

I heard nothing back so I just forgot about it and got on with work. I had risen to the dizzying heights of systems manager and was asked to join a small team to go to Northern Ireland for six months to help turn the "Welworths" stores into "Safeway" stores. Not long after my return, I received a letter saying that if I was still interested in being an extra in the next Bill Baggs classic, I should phone David Rowston, the First Assistant Director. I was on the phone in a flash and a couple of days later I was driving the fifty miles to the location shoot, to begin my career as an extra.

1998 – Auton 2

Early in the morning, complete with my map of the UK (I had no computer, sat nav or mobile phone in 1998), I drove to the location. As I arrived in the little country village that was to be transformed into the site of yet another Auton invasion of the UK, I felt both excited and nervous. This was it, my entry into the real world of films. No matter that it was 'only' a straight to video film aimed at a fan market, it was real film-making and I was about to become an extra. Or so I thought. As I parked the car and looked around the village, I could see no cameras, no sound crew, no cast, no sign of impending alien-inspired doom, nothing. In my nervous anxiety and desperation to be a model of professionalism, I had set off and arrived far too early. I was first on the scene. There followed a couple of hours waiting in the car, during which my nerves settled a little, before the production team of Auton 2 began to arrive, instantly recognisable as the typical

Doctor Who geeks, with whom I had become very familiar at conventions. In truth, despite what I thought at the time, I now happily admit that I was very much a geek myself, despite my nice suit.

Meeting up with various other lost souls and newcomers, we found and duly reported to David Rowston. Incidentally, I had noticed that the sign outside the village church, one of the principal locations for the shoot, proclaimed the vicar to be another Rowston. Looking back, this was no coincidence, merely a good way of finding free locations.

It didn't take long to get to know some of my fellow extras, but I was surprised to find that others didn't want to speak to me. I discovered later that they had been working on this production earlier in the week, and so were now established extras and therefore above us newbies!

It may surprise some readers to discover that this hierarchy among extras, based upon who's been on the set the longest, is still with us today, and is never felt more than on long running shows with regular extras. For example, it was never nice going on "The Bill" as a background policeman due to the unfriendliness of some of the regulars; on "Casualty" the regular extras have their own seating area and woe betide anyone else who sits there. I've been a semi-regular on "Holby City" now for two years and there are still extras who can spend days with me but have still not got around to speaking. To be truthful, I guess those of us who have been regular extras on "Waterloo Road" or even "Scott and Bailey" have sometimes been a little like that but I hope we haven't excluded anyone. It was just that we know each other so well it sometimes seems silly to bond with anyone else coming in new to the show, as it was unlikely that they would be around for more than a day. And if they did stay around, then they might well be stealing our jobs.

I've digressed. Sorry, I'll try to stay focused.

Okay so my first time as an extra pretty much amounted to sitting in the church all day, doing a little screaming and then running out of the church as an imaginary monster started attacking it. I don't remember much more about it, other than getting into a little bit of trouble when I went off to eat my lunch without waiting until I was given permission to do so. However, some excitement was provided by a crew from the Sci-Fi Channel, who turned up to do a behind the scenes documentary. In fact we spent a lot the day just taking photos of the cast and crew. I had loved the first Auton Film and this one looked as if it was going to be even better.

I was so excited when the day was over. I got the photos printed and sent them along with a letter to a science fiction magazine, expressing my love for home-grown low budget British science fiction and complaining that they didn't do enough reviews of such films instead of covering the big blockbusters all the time.

The magazine printed a full page on Auton 2 and they even used my photos. I photocopied it and sent it along with a letter to Bill Baggs to show what I had done to push his movie and to request that when he did Auton 3, I wanted in! Imagine my disappointment when all I got back was a photocopied letter saying, "For all information please see the website."

Remember Michelle who'd gone off to Falmouth to do Media Studies? Well whilst I was still working on the delicatessen counter, her career had moved on. She became a researcher for a local radio station, and then became a news reporter for them. She then moved to be a researcher for local TV and later became a TV presenter and director. At this time she was working on reconstructions of crimes and court proceedings for a local TV show and asked me if I'd like to come in as an extra. How could I refuse? We even got £5 each to buy lunch (although parking in the centre of Bristol cost me £8, so I ended up out of pocket).

Talking to other extras, I learnt of a local agency through which they found work on various TV programmes. I organised some photos and sent them to them.

Meanwhile in my real life with I was asked to go to Basingstoke to meet with the store manager. I went along having no idea what it was he actually wanted of me.

So, on my day off from Frome Safeway I drove to Basingstoke and met up with him.

We sat in the customer canteen and he bought me a coffee and asked how I was getting on as systems Manager in our store, as word had got around that I didn't see eye to eye with the current Frome store manager, (he wasn't wrong there.)

He asked me what salary I would want to transfer to Basingstoke, to manage his delicatessen counter. He knew that I still spent a lot of time out and about in the UK, setting up delicatessen counters in new stores and doing refits, but he wanted me to work for him.

Now, Basingstoke was 60 miles away and I didn't really want the job. It was nice to be asked and it certainly made me feel good about myself, but I had no interest in running a counter full-time any more. I'd left that job behind and moved on into middle management. However in the small world of deli counters, this was a big deal. After all, the counter in Basingstoke was nearly 80 foot long and took the most money of all the delicatessen counters in the country. (There were over 460 at the time).

I was torn. So, not wanting just to say that I wasn't interested, I quoted him a ridiculously high salary, thinking he'd just drop the subject and pay for my breakfast. But to my utter astonishment he agreed immediately.

I had to get out of this right away so I added a comment that should have stopped him in his tracks. I said "Plus travel expenses, of course."

"Fine." he exclaimed without hesitation.

Oops. Now I had accidentally become the highest paid Delicatessen counter manager in the company with the biggest counter and twenty-one members of staff to look after.

Obviously this took up most my time. Who am I kidding? It took over my whole life. My personal life suffered for it in so many ways. As well as splitting from my long term partner, I also had to keep turning TV work down. In fact I often didn't know that I'd been offered it until too late, as I regularly got home at night to find messages on my answer machine about jobs that might have been fun, had I managed to get in touch with the agency earlier. Of course, this was in the days when most people still didn't have mobile phones.

In the end, I only spent a year in Basingstoke and then transferred to a new store back home in Bath. At the same time I was still going from town to town every other week, to open new stores, set up counters and train their staff.

An area trainer's job came up. I was ideally qualified. After all, I knew more about the running of a delicatessen counter than anyone else in the company. That's not showing off, it was just a fact. Every week when new product lines, initiatives and bar-codes were sent down to store I'd be the one updating the information for head office to pass to other stores. With every confidence, I sent in my application. How could they not give me the job?

Somehow, they didn't see it that way, and managed to appoint someone else. I was less than delighted. Then to make matters worse, they asked me to train this person up. My displeasure turned to fury. There I was, 27 years old having been with the company for eleven years. I had always been ready to train and set up when the company needed me but I wasn't good enough for a job that I knew I could do with my eyes shut! I had given up so much for the company. I was so mad in fact that I sat down and wrote a strong e-mail to the head of fresh foods at head office and told him what I thought. (P.S. Thank you Luke Regler my manager for persuading me to do that).

That one e-mail changed my whole life!

I got a letter from the Head of Fresh Foods inviting me to work in London in the Saint Katherine's Dock store on a new initiative. It was only supposed to be a 6 week job but I never went to live back home again. I was then asked to work in the head office in Hayes on a permanent basis, to write training programs and to train everyone from new starters to area managers. This was the job that I was made for. Training is the one job I do best and if it's to do with fresh food or Safeway computer systems then I'm in my element. The truth is that the job took over my whole life for the next few years and as I have promised that this book won't be an autobiography I'll fast forward a tad.

We opened a training centre in the Midlands, in a town called Burton-upon-Trent. I had to look the place up as I'd never heard of it but it turned out to be near Derby.

The houses were so cheap in the North that I sold mine and bought one in Burton. It was only for a year or so while I worked at this centre and after that they planned to open another one in Bristol, so I would be able to go back south again.

I looked up extras agencies in the North of England and joined one in Manchester.

My boss was brilliant and let me do TV work so long as it didn't conflict with my 'real' job.

Coronation Street

In 2002 I did my first episode of Coronation Street. It was really exciting at the time and felt really weird driving the car and heading towards Coronation Street in Manchester.

Extras usually have to wear their own clothes if it's for a production with a contemporary setting. For Corrie the instruction was to bring casual wear, which for me, means a suit with short sleeved shirts. No matter the weather or the occasion I like to wear a suit. The greatest thing about working for Safeway head office was that I got to wear a suit every day of the week. Nice! So, short sleeved shirts and no tie! Does it come any more casual than that? I soon learnt it does!

I turned up to the set and was asked to wait in the extras' room above Audrey's salon as we would be walking around on the street today. "Do you know where that is?" the security guard on the gate asked after he had signed me in and given me an ITV sticker.

It was the only set in the world that I could come to for the first time and actually *know* where all the external locations are, as they are all in exactly the same place as they appear on television.

I put on my sticker with pride and walked up to the street onto the cobbled road. I'll never forget the feeling of coming around the corner by the shop and looking down the street for the first time. Even now I still see it in other people's faces when it's their first time on the Street!

I walked up the street, past the shop, past the houses, past the factory and the garage and headed to Audrey's salon. Sure enough there was a door at the side which lead upstairs to the extras' room, but before I went in I had a good long hard stare at the "Rovers Return"

I don't think you're really an extra until you've done either Corrie or EastEnders!

I went upstairs and sat confidently down in a chair, looking around expectantly, and waiting for someone to tell me that this particular chair belonged to one of the regular extras but no one said anything and everyone seemed very nice. In fact it turned out that it was the first day for quite few other people that day too.

The third Assistant Director (3rd AD) came up to sign us in. I'd had a later start than most of the other extras and we were the second batch that morning. Later we would be walking up and down the street but for now we were told to hang fire as the costume people were coming over to visit us.

Fifteen minutes later a middle aged lady came in and asked who the later extras were. We put our hands up and she asked one of the woman extras to get out the clothes that she had brought for today. The lady did so and the costume woman declared her satisfaction with what she saw. I sat and awaited my turn, wondering if I would be allowed to wear my suit or if it would have to be the short sleeved shirt.

The costume lady spoke to the next person and again was very happy with what they had brought in. To be fair it wasn't difficult as she had phoned us all in advance to tell us to be casual with no bright colours and no stripes or logos and although this was March we were to dress as if it were May!

Upon my turn, I proudly unzipped my suit bag. "Have you got anything casual?" she asked after rifling through my clothes?

"These are casual," I replied. "They're all short sleeved shirts and some of them you wouldn't even wear a tie with!"

She proceeded to explain that this was not casual and that I should have brought T-shirts and jeans with trainers!

"Oh, you mean scruffy clothes," I told her. I didn't own any of them.

She wasn't at all happy, but still left me with the suit and a short sleeved shirt.

Later, when extras were picked for each scene I found myself left behind every time and by late afternoon I'd guessed that the costume lady had told the 3rd AD. that she wasn't happy with my wardrobe. Although he had been perfectly nice to me, he just wasn't going to use me. So, I never got to be on Corrie that first day. To make things worse, it was a multi-episode day which means that they film several scenes next to each other for different episodes, which would have meant more money.

I'd learnt a lesson. That was when I discovered "Primark" and Asda "George", sellers of cheap clothes with no logos; that might have just have been invented especially for Television and film work.

For my next few jobs I had to go out and buy a whole bunch of what I'd call "Corrie Clothes" or in other words, very casual wear!

For the next year or so I didn't do a lot of TV work due to my Training day job which was a whole new concept for the company. So my boss and I had to write many new company procedures from scratch while also working with new store equipment and writing new training programs for them. What TV work I did was mostly on Hollyoaks, Coronation Street or Emmerdale. I don't know why but for the next few years all I ever seemed to do on Emmerdale was to play a doctor! To this day I have never managed to visit the village.

July 2004

With the rumours of a corporate take-over at Safeway, the training budget was cut almost overnight, and I was on the move again, firstly back to the West Midlands as a delicatessen trainer and then back to London, where I spent a year living in a hotel near Heathrow, with another change to my job. I was now working with the company's Head of Delicatessen retail operations manager.

Now at last I was working at a level where I was free to do all the things I ever wanted to with the department for the whole company. I even got to write the company procedure book on computer based ordering systems for the delicatessen. (Oh my lord how boring and geekish I sound, but it had been an ambition of mine for years).

My new boss and I had a brilliant time working together although we were very different in our working methods. She could think on her feet and could get crazy ideas that were so 'out of the box', whereas I was the more grounded and methodical one who knew all the rules about the products we sold, sales data and working methods of the counter.

We would take it in turns to write monthly company delicatessen news books promoting new and fresh ideas, new products and merchandising plans, new equipment and money making ideas. It was a brilliant working partnership but alas, as with all things, it came to an end when Morrison's took the company over and handed out redundancy letters to all 1500 of us in the Hayes head office.

Now, during my time at Delicatessen Retail Operations I was told that I had been allocated a budget of £30,000 a year to spend on internal corporate and training films, which I had to spend, or the budget would be lost. What an opportunity! I was being paid to do something I enjoyed and could now combine it with my dream job!

I wrote a 5 part training film and hired a crew to film, edit and duplicate it, whilst I set up the film. I got hold of all my favourite delicatessen managers from all around the country and brought them to Bath for filming, (again a good excuse to go home and get paid for the inconvenience).

The film wasn't all that good to be fair but it was a great way to get experience. It didn't matter all that much either, as the company was in the middle of being taken over, and within months all our policies and procedures would be meaningless anyway.

Then the day arrived when we in the Fresh Food Operations Department got our redundancy notices. The fear that had been hanging over us finally became a reality. I had joined Safeway in 1988 when I was 16 years old and had never had to go outside into the real word for a job. I was terrified.

I had heard rumours that Morrison's were looking for someone with experience to make internal training films for the company. Now that they were acquiring Safeway they needed a quick way to communicate information to all the stores and help turn us all into one company as soon as possible. It was a permanent position, but the requirements were rather demanding. The successful applicant would have experience of retail training and training course writing as well as having the camera and editing skills that were needed actually to do the job! It was made for me. I applied, got an interview and was taken on right away with the same salary, bonuses, perks and the like that I had had from Safeway. I even kept the company car and petrol allowance, although I would be primarily based at home!

I couldn't have wished for a better job. My new boss was amazing and so good to me considering the attitude I had. Looking back on it, the takeover had changed me in ways that I now regret. I had become obnoxious and rude and although the redundancy package was amazing I had become too scared to enter the real world. So I took this job with a one year option to take the package.

My first task was to make a film about the 'Company 20 Basics'. It was the first training film I had made from scratch all the way to distribution and I wasn't very happy with the end result, although in my defence, I was also hindered by the fact that head-office (now based in Bradford) made changes to it, simply because it affected so many people who all had to have their say in the final result, some contradicting others in the feedback and the changes that they demanded. I would have liked the opportunity to remake it later, but I never did get that chance.

My boss was amazing, always accommodating my requests to change my days off, so long as it didn't affect my filming schedules.

At this point in my life I had everything I could ever want and the great thing was that I knew this and appreciated it everyday.

I loved making films. I didn't care what they were about. I loved researching the subject matter, writing the script, finding the locations, filming, lighting, editing, and duplicating the finished product.

An old friend of mine, who also lived in Bath, became my voice-over artist so it was great to go home and see him and catch up. He was (and is still very much) a Doctor Who fan and we had heard that the BBC were getting all the rights back to start a new series. How many times had we heard this before?

I made films about cleaning chicken ovens, assembling fish counters, and countless health and safety films for stores, warehouses, vehicle maintenance units, transport departments, processing factories and even the slaughter house. The fascinating possibilities were endless. I was saving the company a fortune by being paid a single salary and utilising all the people we had in the company.

But I still got a thrill from being on real film sets where they were spending so much money using equipment that I couldn't imagine ever getting to use for my own films.

But back to my job as an extra... One day I got a call to do a McDonalds commercial near Manchester. It was the coldest day EVER! It had snowed overnight and we all turned up in hats and scarves (as you would), about thirty of us in all. We were sent onto the bus.

Have I explained the extras bus yet? No? Well, if you ever see a film set do look out for the really old rubbish looking 1960s style bus. That's where the extras sit all day. Usually the heating doesn't work, the seats are falling apart and someone always leaves the door open.

Anyway, we were on this bus and the AD explained that we had got Stuart Hall from "It's a Knock-out" on set today and when we went out, we would be put into teams of three.

This was seven o'clock in the morning and there was snow everywhere. He then went on to say that the commercial would be for the summer so we were waiting for the snow to melt and we would not be allowed to take coats, hats or scarves out when we were filming

It was going to be a long morning. The great thing in those days was that there were only a limited number of us doing extra work and we all knew each other well. So it was no great chore just to sit and chat all morning.

After lunch the snow had pretty much gone and we were sent outside.

"When Stuart Hall comes up to you, please act as if you don't care what he's saying to you and don't react too much."

Not a difficult instruction but you'd be surprised how many people didn't actually understand it!

We got ourselves into teams of three and Stuart came along saying things like" Come on get excited, it's time to get really excited – come on!"

Most people would do exactly what he said and get really excited, screaming and jumping on him.

When it came to our turn, not only had we taken in what the AD had actually asked us to do (about six times now, as each successive team had made a mess of it), but we were so cold that there was no way we could get excited even if we really wanted to.

We did the scene, failing to get excited as requested and got paid £90 for the privilege (minus agency fees!)

Now there were about 15 teams of 3 and we all did the same thing but we were told that of all the teams, only one would be used in the commercial.

A few months later the advert came on the TV on prime-time between the soaps and there we were, right in the centre shot. I was getting text messages from everyone I knew informing me that I was on TV. I'd never had this much exposure and it was so weird that people all around the country had seen me. I'd visit a store and the deli (who usually knew me) would say they'd seen me on the Television. How jolly exciting!

Of course looking back, I should have asked for more money but I didn't really care nor need the money back then. How things have changed!

One day I was doing Coronation Street. We were filming some scenes on a set of a pub called the Weatherfield Arms. I don't think they ever actually showed an exterior of this pub. They certainly hadn't built one because it was based in one of the stages with the Old Italian restaurant set.

We were told it was going to be a really long day, so to save a bit of money, I had found a cheaper car park, (yes we have to pay for parking and even lunch on Corrie). Anyway, when I arrived at this car park nice and early, the chap asked me how long I would be there, as they block other cars in to get as much out of the car park as possible. "Well" I said "I'm here all day." So I left my keys with them and walked to the studio.

I signed in and went in for a coffee. There was my friend Lenny. Lenny is brilliant. He's a massive bald black guy with the heart of a kitten!

We were sitting in the coffee area when young Sam Aston came along who plays Chesney Brown and said to Lenny "Wow, look at the size of your muscles" Lenny flexed them for him and Sam seemed impressed at first but then he looked at Lenny and just asked "Have you got 50p for the drink machine?"

I was very amused by the cheek of it but he was such a lovely kid.

That reminds me. There used to be a breakfast van behind the street set for the crew and actors but not for extras. If we wanted breakfast we had to go to the canteen at Granada and pay for it! Even so, we used to go to the van whenever we could get away with it and acting very confidently we would order a bacon butty, which was quick to make thus allowing us to escape before too many questions were asked.

"You crew? "They would ask.

"Yes, I'm on dailies" is all we would have to say. It usually worked.

Well, on this particular day we ended up only doing one scene in the Weatherfield arms and that was it. We were wrapped before ten o'clock in the morning, so I had to go and get my car back. I had said that I would be away all day and so they had barricaded it in, right in the corner. It must have taken twenty minutes of moving all the other cars around just to get it out. Needless to say I never parked there again.

I got home by lunch time and the phone rang. It was my Manchester agent. (Before I forget to mention, the rule up North as in Manchester, Liverpool, Leeds and Bradford is that you can only be with one agent within a 60 mile radius. Not an issue if you do extra work just for fun, but a real problem if you do it for a living).

"John", my agent asked, "did you do Coronation Street this morning?"

"Yes." I replied assuming that they had complained about something I'd done. Had I been seen taking photos of the street? I was sure I'd done it out of the way of the security cameras, or had I been caught getting a free breakfast?

Have I mentioned the many rules of being an extra? Okay, well an extra is the lowest link in the line of command on set.

Some people struggle to deal with this concept hence the whole "I've been here longer than you" thing that goes on.

Being an extra is simple. Anyone can do it. The whole cast and crew knows that anyone can do it and that you do not need to be qualified or have any experience in doing it.

An extra is simply a prop. A prop to be moved around when needed to add a little life or colour to a scene.

The only difference between an extra and a prop is that we eat more and we breathe, oh and we tend to moan a lot!

Some extras don't like the word "extra" but I'll go into that later.

An extra's job is simply to do as they are told, to keep everyone happy and to keep quiet until it's time to go home.

No one has any respect for extras except for people outside the industry altogether. And even this is usually only because the extra has been in some show that they happen to watch on TV.

I have digressed again, but it needed to be understood. Anyway, as I was saying, my Manchester agent had called and asked if I'd been working on Coronation Street that morning. (As if she didn't know, as it was she who had booked me).

She told me that the 2nd AD had been on the phone (the person who books the extras with the agency) and had said that the crew had been so impressed with us that morning that they would like us to become regulars in the Weatherfield arms.

Wow, now that's a compliment! I had obviously done my "holding a beer glass" and my "pretending to talk" very well that morning. More likely it was just that we had kept our mouths shut and got on with the one scene, (and had got away with the free breakfast).

We did a few episodes in the Weatherfield until one day Lenny was an hour late.

We usually get there, sign in at the gate and sit around waiting for the 3rd AD to sign us in. This can often take as much as an hour.

Anyway, that day Lenny got in very flustered. "I just got a call from the agent" he said. Apparently she hadn't been very happy at being woken up before eight o'clock and having to call Lenny to ask where he was!

"So, where were you?" I asked

"Well, I just figured that as they never sign us in on time I might as well not come in for an hour. So I had an extra lie in bed!"

He hadn't told the agent this but when he turned up to set the AD went ballistic at him. As I said earlier we just need to turn up on time and do as we're told. Follow those rules and anyone can do it.

Poor Lenny

21st April 2005 Flyboys

This was my very first time on a big movie and one of the few films I've been in that I've taken the time to watch. It's a shame it didn't do very well as it's a brilliant movie but I'm sure it'll be "discovered" at some point in the future.

It was a big crowd scene and we spent the day at the train station just milling around whilst the actors did their bit. I've just gone through the photos of this day and for some reason can't remember much of it but wanted to include it in here as it was my first big extra call, with over two hundred extras.

Having been used to small sets and bases, this one was weird because when I arrived there were so many big marquees but I eventually found the one marked "Background" (another word for extras) and went inside.

It looked chaotic with hundreds of extras running around in different costumes from the First World War.

There were several 3rd ADs on set and it took ages to set up every scene but that's about all I can remember. I think I was so blown away by the sheer scale of it and how they'd turned this regular modern train station into one of the period.

2005 - Hollyoaks

I used to do Hollyoaks so often and played just about every role you could think of in the show: chef, policeman, waiter, diner, drinker, paramedic (I'll mention that story later),CID officer, teacher, parent, doctor (too many times to count), estate agent, reporter even a student once. On this particular day I was a driving instructor, teaching the McQueens' mum to drive.

We had spent the whole day together in the car. Back then, to my shame I was a smoker but always tried to be considerate of other people who didn't smoke.

I had known I was going to be in this car for most of the day so I hadn't had a cigarette all morning and was waiting until lunch time.

We had a nice time in the car together just chatting about anything. She even told me that there was a job going for an actor of about my age on the show, and had offered to ask about it for me. How nice was that? I did point out that I was just an extra and that extras can't act (otherwise they would be actors).

I made two big mistakes that day. One was that during the conversation about acting I said that I could never cry on demand in the way that I had seen many actors doing. How could anyone call themselves an actor if they couldn't even cry on demand? I had asked.

This obviously struck home with her. We went to lunch, where I got to see Jimmy McKenna who's the best thing about Hollyoaks, as he's in the film Highlander (which I adore)!

At lunch I could hold out no longer and simply had to have a cigarette. I ate some mints to mask the smell, but as everyone knows, mints do not work.

Lunch over; we went back into the car. She went ballistic with me "Have you had a cigarette?"

"Yes," I replied feebly, "but I had a mint"

"I can't believe you would do that to your fellow actor, how could you smoke a cigarette knowing you're coming back into the car with me. You have no respect for your fellow thespian?"

I was so embarrassed. After spending the morning with an actress who was treating me as an equal, despite the fact that I was only extra, I had to go and ruin everything by smoking.

Did I say I'd made two mistakes? Well you'll recall I had aired my opinion on actors who cannot cry on demand. Not having seen the script, I had no idea that she was meant to cry at the end of the scene.

The 1st AD came along and asked her, "Would you like a tear-stick?"

"No I'll be okay."

I realised straight away that she had only said that because of my earlier comments and I felt really bad, sitting there just willing her to take the tear stick and be done with it.

She couldn't cry. The longer it went on, the worse the situation became. There is never any time to waste on daily TV soaps and it's absolutely not a sign of a bad actor to use a tear stick. It's just about the turnaround time to shoot the scene and get onto the next one.

I watched this episode when it aired and it turned out in the story that my character had asked her daughter out on a date three times already whilst they were in the cafe! Nice to see I got to play another slimy character without even knowing it.

25/26th May 2005- Pontins TV commercial

I'd gone to a casting for a TV advert as a "dad" but not really being a dad-looking chap, I didn't really expect to get the role. Anyway in the casting session, I had to sit in a chair pretending to drive a car and getting angry with the driver next to me. I had to do my 'concentrating' face, which looks pretty evil but I did it. I didn't expect to hear anything about it but to my surprise they rang the next day to say that I'd got the part!

Extra Time

I had to go out and buy a bunch of colourful summer clothes as these were items I'd never used on set before. I was pretty excited but hadn't asked about the money. Money was never really that important to me back then and I simply assumed that it would be a couple of thousand pounds.

When the agency called me with the location and times I asked how much I was getting. It was £150 a day for a complete buyout! £300 minus twenty per cent for advert agency fees! Rubbish

Well the big day came and I was getting to spend the night at Pontins. I was looking forward to meeting my wife and kids.

The first location was a blighter to find as it was in the middle of nowhere but I still managed to get there early.

The crew were really nice. It's amazing how different you get treated when there are no actors on set.

I met a chap in the green room and asked him if he was doing another advert.

"I'm the main Dad in the Pontins Go-kart commercial." He replied.

"But that's what I am?" and then it clicked. He must just be the other guy that I race against in front of my TV family. Talking of which I'd not met my TV wife yet.

Well imagine both of our surprises when we were called out on set and it seemed that neither of us were getting a wife even though we both had a child! What sort of Pontins advert is this? Are we a couple or what? No-one seemed to know the answer to that question.

37

The advert was filmed in two parts. In the first half the two dads (?) raced against each other outside their house in two toy tractors. It was funny, but once we were outside on set I soon realised that I wasn't quite the main actor, as I had been led to believe. It was split between the two of us.

It was lucky that I'd gone out and spent lots of money on clothes as the other guy ended up wearing my clothes too! (I didn't get any extra money for lending clothes).

After the first day we were given a map and told to make our way to Pontins to spend the night.

Well, I don't really know what I expected but staying in Pontins was very much like being put in jail (I imagine) as the rooms were just big square boxes with big patio doors and a number printed in large lettering on the front!

It was so boring that we (the two 'dads' and the kids' parents) decided to get together for a drink in one of the rooms. I'm afraid I drank a tad too much, (in my case that's one glass), and ended up making a mistake I'll never make again. The other 'dad' asked me how much I was getting for the job, so I told him, thinking he must be on loads more than me. It couldn't really be any less than what I was earning. But it was!! He had come through a different agency and was earning half of what I was.-Never Talk Money!

The next day we got to ride the go-karts, the point of the advert being not to have a rubbish time at home with your rubbish cars but to come to exciting Pontins and have a brilliant time with real go-karts. I was so looking forward to this as we had the go-kart track all to ourselves. All we had to do was to make it look like we were having an amazing time.

At first it was absolutely brilliant as we went round and round laughing and shouting at each other, with about thirty crew on the outside and a bunch of extras (unpaid residents) at the other end.

The first fifteen minutes was fun but going around and around and laughing non-stop does take a lot out of you.

We must have been going for about two hours! It soon stopped being fun and I went from not wanting to be anywhere else but on these go-karts to not caring where in the world I was so long as it was somewhere else!

The 'first' started shouting at me "John, smile! Smile John! You're having fun so show it!" He was really shouting.

I tried to smile but the face wouldn't have it. My facial muscles had ceased to work ages ago, when I'd run out of smiles and shouting.

How can smiling be so difficult? Well the only way to get any sort of natural smile now was to laugh. I just went round laughing and laughing. It sounded weird because I wasn't really laughing but by laughing I was able to get my mouth to look more like a natural smile. It was tough.

I'm sure Pontins is in fact a really good fun place to go if you are with family and friends. I just had a bad time as I didn't know anyone.

The only time a stranger has ever (to this day) recognised me off the TV was in Manchester a good few months later when this girl came up to me and asked "Excuse me but are you the guy off the Pontins advert?"

I was shocked! Not just because someone had recognised me off the TV but also that this advert was being shown but I hadn't seen it!

Instead of saying "yes that's me", I asked, "Is it on TV? What channel and when?"

I also heard from someone else that it was being shown on one of the satellite children's channels so I spent weeks trying to catch it. I never saw it but did get quite into Sponge Bob in the process.

I had kept a call-sheet so I contacted the production company to say that I was in their advert and had still not seen it. They said they'd be happy to send me a copy, for £30! This was back when I was still looking for my TV stuff so I paid it and got a DVD in the mail. Our bit was only about 12 seconds long!

9th June 2005 – Life on Mars

Up to now I had been very passive in my career as an extra, accepting whatever work was offered to me, taking pride in never being late and in never saying no. The first show that I actually chased was Life on Mars. The show first caught my attention when I read about it in a magazine. It sounded a little bit science fiction concerning, as it did, a man from 2006 getting sent back to 1973.

I went to see my booker in Manchester and asked if I could get on it and it proved to be no problem for them at all. The one great advantage about being in anything that's not set in contemporary times is that we get to dress up, so we don't have to take loads of clothes with us.

I arrived at the location and parked up next to an old brown Cortina, which it turned out, would become famous as Gene Hunt's car. With hindsight I so wish that I had had my photo taken next to it.

We were sent to costume and there on the rack I found a fabulous set of 1970s clothes with my name on.

It wasn't much of a scene as all we were doing was waiting to get into a club. Everyone had a girlfriend to stand with, but mine got sent to a passing car so I ended waiting with another left over man.

It wasn't particularly exciting but I was just glad to get on the show.

17th June 2005 - Flyboys

Then it was back to Flyboys again. We had been invited back and told that we would have two weeks work on the production. I had to take an emergency holiday from work but the weather was great and I would enjoy two weeks on the film.

On this particular day we were being attacked by a plane. I was a French military captain with my own fun platoon.

Now, when an extra gets stripes or appears to be in charge, it's not because they are any better than anyone else, it's simply because they look right or have the right build for the costume. Some extras get confused and think that they have been singled out as being special but it's simply because they fit the costume!

As the costume for the soldier in charge of this unit fitted me, I got to have a gun! I'd never used one before so I had to attend my own training session on how to use, load, fire and hold a gun safely and convincingly.

Our unit ended up being one little bit of a massive scene and we were pretty much at the edge of frame.

The scene involved a plane coming down to shoot at us and then another plane chasing that one away. Rehearsing this felt rather silly. We were told that there would be explosions and squibs (bullet explosions) and so we shouldn't wander about near where the flags were, which was where the squibs had been put. I was told to fire my gun towards the plane but not actually to aim directly at it, as gunpowder can fly out and be dangerous. We rehearsed several times but without the plane or the explosions and it simply felt stupid.

Then it was time for the first take. There were so many cameras everywhere and we had been told to stay in character until we hear the word cut.

So they turned over (set the cameras and sound to record) and called action. Our unit walked into the scene and then a real plane came down towards us, it got lower and lower and everyone started to shout, my guys were running all over the place for cover but I had been told to stand there and shoot at the plane.

It came down so seriously low that I thought it would land on top of us, the noise was deafening and then the squibs went off!

Dirt and debris was thrown up into the air and several trucks exploded. Men burst into flames and fell off the raised road onto the blue mat.

I held my ground and fired at the plane. I used up all my shots and it then came back for a second pass, I dived for cover at this point as I was out of ammunition.

So much for feeling stupid, we were no longer acting and this all felt far too real for my liking. It was so weird.

We ended up doing the same scene six times for six different camera set-ups, but the oddest part was when they wanted to get the view from the attacking plane. The plane was replaced with a big black camera helicopter. I was reminded again to make sure I did not fire directly at the helicopter as I could damage the lens, which shows just how low to the ground it came.

On every set up, there was never any need to be asked to keep the energy up as each time was just as exciting as the first.

2005 – Doctor Who; The Christmas Invasion

I don't remember the exact date of my first day on Doctor Who, which is weird as it was one of the greatest days of my life. But I do remember that it all started one day, when I was on an episode of Dalziel and Pascoe. I got a call to ask if I'd like to do three days on Doctor Who. This was my chance finally to do the one job (other than Highlander – did I mention how much I loved that show?) that I would have done anything to get. They wanted to pay me money to be on Doctor Who. Weird – and fantastic, as Christopher Eccleston's Doctor would have said, although he had departed the show by now, the first season having just finished on TV with Eccleston regenerating into David Tennant. They wanted me for three days on the Christmas Special playing a member of UNIT inside the Tower of London

Base (to be filmed at the Millennium Stadium in Cardiff). So, what do you think I said? Unbelievably, I had to say that I could only do one of the three days, as I was very busy with my day job and there was no way my boss would allow me to take three days off. That was no good to them. I had lost the chance to be on Doctor Who.

Later that day they called back. "Which one day are you available?" I told them and couldn't believe it when they said that they could fit me in. I was so excited.

On the day I was so stupidly early, that I had to sit in the extras bus for ages before the crew finally arrived.

Then more extras arrived, none of whom seemed as excited as I was. Where were all the Who fans?

The Third AD came onto the bus to see us and made a seriously big deal about cameras and photos, saying that if anyone even took out of their pocket a phone that he thought might contain a camera (not all phones did back then) he would send them off set! It was at this point that I decided that I had better put my camera away into my bag! I was only wearing my work suit but I'd been given a UNIT badge with my photo on it, so I really wanted a photo with that on!

I waited on the bus most of the morning but finally got called to set, which was inside the Millennium stadium, where one corner had been set up as the UNIT Base Command. As I sat there looking around I turned my head round to the other corner behind me and behold it was the location from the previous year's episode "Dalek" where all the soldiers had shot at the Dalek.

Lunch was called and I still hadn't been used.

After the break the scene being filmed was the mass exodus of the control room by the UNIT personnel who had had their minds taken over by the Sycorax. So all those picked from the last scene and all of us new people had to be "affected by some alien device".

The scene was simply us walking (almost trance like) down a corridor while the actors shouted at each other. The external scenes were being filmed on location in London.

I didn't mind the fact that I wasn't seen or didn't spend much time on set; it was just the fact that I had finally made it onto Doctor Who.

On the way out, the security man took my UNIT badge.

19th/ 20th June 2005- Life on Mars

I was lucky enough to be invited back to Life on Mars for a couple of days to play one of the local drinkers in a pub called the "Trafford Arms"

Some of the guys had wigs put on them. I was hoping to get one too as I had a very un-70s style short hair.

All the usual crowd were there, about forty of us, who I'd see on most of the jobs that I'd done, so it was great to catch up.

Although we were allocated clothes we could choose what shoes to wear, so when I saw this pink pair with pink ribbons for laces I simply had to have them.

One of the things I found funny about getting onto the 1970s set with our 70s clothes was the fact that we all had our mobile phones stuffed in our pockets!

I spoke to one of the crew who'd seen a finished version of the first episode, as I had said that I was looking forward to the show. He told me that the first episode looked amazing but corrected me when I called it science fiction. To this day I would still call it sci-fi. After all, it's about a man who has travelled in time!!

4th/5th September 2005 Doctor Who – New Earth

I got a call to go back onto Doctor who and, rather excitingly, I was asked if I minded wearing prosthetics. Of course I jumped at it.

At this time I had a goatee beard but found that I was being asked to shave it off for a lot of shows, not this time however.

When we got to base I was told to wait in the bus as they had brought in a choreographer to teach us the movements!

As the other extras turned up this information was passed on, somehow turning into a rumour that we were having a dance lesson. Extras' rumours are brilliant. We are rarely told anything, so someone will make something up which quickly becomes established fact for the rest of the day. Oh my lord, I cannot dance to save my life!

Extra Time

We were introduced to a fantastic and lovely lady called Alisa Berk who had done a lot of skin work on TV and film and is now the choreographer on Doctor Who.

Alisa informed us that we were to be playing hospital patients suffering from every single disease in the universe. We had been kept in some sort of cryogenic freezer so this would be the first time that we would walk, so we needed to be stiff boned - but not to walk like zombies.

So much for the dance rehearsal! It was a training session on walking as a Doctor Who patient.

We did two set-ups that they thought we might film. One was when the Doctor walks out of the lift and we all go towards him and the other was when we were let out of the freezers for the first time.

On the first set-up four "Hero" patients were picked to be in front. I was not one of these. (Note: a hero extra is not in fact a hero in the story as extras are simply extras and are never the hero, but they may get a close up and get paid a little more money for being featured more. They therefore need to have more paid attention to make-up and costume).

For our costumes they gave us big grey nighties. Apart from that we were allowed to keep our pants on but that was all.

When we went back to base to get make-up and costume done, one of the hero extras was talking to the make-up lady, refusing to cut his beard off. The upshot was that he was sacked as a hero patient and they asked me to take his place, so long as I was willing to take my beard off. They didn't have to ask twice. I went straight to the honey wagon (toilets) and shaved it off there and then.

So, four of us became hero patients and had to have special close-up make-up, boils and lumps on our faces which, unlike with the "regular" make up, were put on one at a time rather than in little "bundles of boils". It took an hour and a half to apply and then our arms and legs were sprayed to show the veins, as we were not supposed to have ever seen the sun.

As we were getting onto the bus to take us onto set, I saw a cat woman getting into the back of a car. I guessed she was with us.

We spent the journey making faces at the passing cars thinking we could scare the drivers but no one took any notice. It wasn't until we got off the bus that we realised that it had blacked out windows.

The location was the Millennium Centre, a big opera house and concert venue in Cardiff, in which we were just using the large foyer. It was a night shoot and so cold! We had brought our clothes with us as we were told we would be signing out on location.

I finally got to see David Tennant as the Doctor as he hadn't been on set when we filmed the Christmas special. He was so nice to everyone and spoke to all the extras saying hello and asking where they were from. I liked him immediately. That's all it takes for me to take to an actor, for them to acknowledge us - it doesn't have to be any more than a nod. A lot of actors or the crew don't like talking to extras. In fact animals usually get more respect on set. To be a successful extra, you have to give up quite a lot of your self-respect, so when something brilliant happens, such as an actor noticing that you are actually a real person, you take it to heart and don't forget it.

Extra Time

Billie Piper was on set too and I had managed to piece together enough information to understand what was going on in the story.

We rehearsed the scene where we went into the lift, which was just a wooden prop, meaning that we could only film it one way.

When this scene was done it was back on the bus and then lunch. It's weird sometimes having breakfast at six in the evening and lunch at two in the morning. This was one of those two o'clock in the morning lunches.

Unlike on The Christmas Invasion, no one had specifically mentioned that personal cameras were banned on this episode, but we all knew better than ever to get one out on set. However, something that extras tend to do is to take pictures of each other away from set. Even then, if we are in anything other than contemporary clothes, if we are in special costumes or make-up, we know better than to put photos on the internet until the show has been broadcast.

We spent lunch laughing at each other's faces and taking photos of each other on the extras' bus.

Then we were taken back to location and the four "hero" extras were taken outside one at a time and wetted down with cold water! It was freezing.

The scene took place after we had been drenched with the decontamination fluid. We were now leaving the lift, one at a time and touching each other, spreading the cure to all our diseases. The one thing I actually remember the first AD saying to me when it was my turn, was to go a second time but to slow down so that my mother would recognise me when it was on TV.

I did as requested but what he neglected to tell me was that they were only filming me from my neck down. Another thing an extra must know is that even if you are being featured or even if you have a line to speak please, don't assume for one minute that your speaking role will definitely be on TV, until you've actually seen it. I've had so many cut lines and heard so many similar stories from other extras.

After this scene we were told to go upstairs to the changing rooms (we were still on location), and get showered. I was a little baffled because I couldn't figure out when they were going to do the reverse shot of us in the decontamination lift and why were we getting showered on location rather than back on base.

We went upstairs in little groups and queued for the costume department who were taking our prosthetics off one at a time.

I was even more confused when we were told to get back into costume and see make-up, after we'd been showered and cleaned up. This was weird.

I went to see costume again and they put just a few red marks on my face, as if I had been cured of the diseases!

We went back down to set and the next scene was The Doctor telling Rose how he had cured us. I was put into place and told to look as if we had never seen the world before. Everything was all new and we were like children. There I was, filming a scene with David Tennant! David grabbed me and I gazed at him in adoring gratitude, thinking that I was doing my best ever acting for Doctor Who. When I saw the scene when it was broadcast, I realized to my shame and disappointment that all I had managed to achieve was to look completely gormless and confused. This was another reminder that extras can't act. If they could act, they would be actors, but they are not and should never be given acting roles, even if it is only a facial expression.

There was one more set up to do which required all the extras to stand still in specific places so that the camera could multiply us for a big wide shot where it looks as if the room is filled with patients and Cat Nuns.

We were wrapped but made aware that we were coming back soon for some more patient scenes.

14th September 2005 – Hollyoaks

I was booked to play a slimy reporter on Hollyoaks and although it's not a show I have ever watched, it was work. Furthermore, it's a well-known fact that everyone who does Hollyoaks gets to play a speaking roles at some point.

On this particular day it was my turn.

All I had to do was cross the road and go up to one of the actresses and ask her something about an impending trial.

I was asked to start the top of the scene with a cigarette. The prop guy had some fake ones, if I wanted, but I was given the option of smoking for real if I preferred, using my own cigarettes.

It seemed easy enough and we did a take. I was too slow crossing the road. Take two and another cigarette. This time I was too fast crossing the road, another cigarette. Another take and something else was wrong. Altogether, we must have done about seven takes and in the end I simply had to start the scene with the cigarette unlit, as even I couldn't smoke that much. I have never agreed to use a real cigarette in a scene since.

On the same day I was allowed to wait inside, in the warm, with the actors (simply because I got to say a couple of lines). I was sitting there with a pretty well-known guest actress who was chatting away with me, probably not realising that I was just an extra. Most extras would keep their mouth shut in this situation and I did just that. Well this actress (who shall remain nameless) told me that her nephew had asked if he could take a photo of her and make it look like she knew nothing about it and then send it to "Heat" magazine for the section of "Spotted Stars in Public Places". He earned himself £200 for it! I loved that story. Brilliant! She got free press and he earned some cash.

16th September 2005 – Hollyoaks Let loose

Hollyoaks Let Loose was a short-lived, late night spin-off of Hollyoaks and wasn't that good. (In my opinion, the "Hollyoaks in the City" series has been the best spin off of the show to date).

Two Days after being a slimy reporter on Hollyoaks, I was asked to be in the spin-off series, which was a little surprising as usually we're not allowed to be in the same show playing a different person until a good few weeks have passed. So, I tried to look after the integrity of show by shaving my beard off again. (I don't know why I made the effort, as they knew I'd just done main Hollyoaks but that didn't seem to bother anyone but me).

When I got to the set the same old group of extras were all there. This was still a brilliant time to do 'background' (another word for what extras do) as it was always the same bunch of people playing different roles in different shows. I actually had a TV wife who wasn't my real partner, who in real life was married with two children. Monica was always booked with me and we were cast as a TV married couple so often. Then there was that crazy taxi driver, Mark and of course my Coronation Street Weatherfield Arms fellow regular Lenny. They were all there this day, so it wasn't going to matter what the weather was like or how much we did, it was just going to be a fun day.

The location was a house that belonged to Phil Redmond, the creator of Hollyoaks as well as Brookside and Grange Hill. We were supposed to be at a party.

In the scene Mark and I had an especially good time, stealing Lenny's hat, and Mark just didn't want to stop singing "For He's a Jolly Good Fellow", even after the rest of us had stopped. He had already managed to piss off the third AD by asking if we would get more money for singing and threatening to mime if we didn't get it.

The AD mustn't have found us funny as he then decided to do the next scene with all thirty extras except for Mark and myself who were kept in the kitchen out of the way. I think this was to calm us down and teach us a lesson.

We didn't do anything on set all afternoon while everybody else got to pretend to party.

Finally hours later we were told we could go onto set but asked to stay at the back of the room as it would ruin continuity if we were seen, as the room had now been established without us.

Mark was still in a silly mood and bet me that he could get closer to the camera than I could. At this point I wanted to be on my best behaviour. The last thing we wanted was for someone to complain about us to the agency, but how could I possibly let him win that game?

The next scene started and we were at the back as requested but then the third (3rd AD) left the room so as not to be in shot himself. Mark was half way down the other end with the actors and the camera crew before I'd even noticed he'd gone.

They cut the scene that they were filming from that angle and I knew I had only one chance of beating him. So, just before they were ready to shoot again, I moved my start position closer to the action and as soon as they turned over I moved like the wind down to the action.

We were all told then to keep our positions. I was worried that the third might come back in and notice that I was right next to all the actors and not at the back of the room where he had told us to stay. *(Is now a good time to mention that I've never been this naughty since? I've become a well behaved extra now).* Mark wasn't far behind me but there was no way that I'd let him win. To cap off the whole thing, we had been told to stay where we were so that a hand-held camera could be brought out to be the actress's POV *(Point of View. Pretty much the only time we can look into a camera lens is when it's a POV shot, as the camera shows what the actor or actress is supposed to be seeing).*

The POV shot went to all of the actors' faces one by one and then to the nearby extras. I got my own POV, full on face right in the camera and won the game of who could get closest to camera hands down.

Mark and I should never be booked on the same job together but we always were!

22nd September 2005 – Hollyoaks Let Loose

We were called back to do a continuity scene for the show at the same location, but when we turned up we soon realised they were filming the same party as before but nearly a week later. When I say it was the same party in the same show I also mean they were the same open bottles of stale alcohol-free beer and the same six-day-old sandwiches and food on the table!

The only reason I mention this day is because Hollyoaks is filmed in Liverpool which was over ninety miles from my house. I travelled all the way there and back just for one scene, which didn't even involve me!

The camera was facing one particular actor and I was asked to come in and stand on the edge of the scene, on the left, out in the doorway. I couldn't figure out why as the camera wasn't facing me and I'd been pretty much on my best behaviour today even though Mark was there.

Then I was being told, "Go back a little, a little more… OK that's it. You're now blocking the light off the actors face!"

That was it. I was just being used to block the light off an actor. They could have used a piece of cardboard on a stand, but no. I was doing the job of a piece of cardboard. Well worth the trip.

I never took it to heart as after all, I had a real job and this was just a bit of fun, but as I said earlier, you do need to lose any sort of self-respect or delusions of grandeur as an extra.

1st October 2005 – Trevor McDonald tonight

I'd had a call to ask if I wouldn't mind playing a rapist in a crime reconstruction. I was cool with it as it's just TV and not real life.

I went to the location at some abandoned hospital in Manchester, (you would be surprised just how many of those I've been to), and was put through make-up. They had a photo of the real perpetrator and they made my eyes up to kind of match his.

The weird thing with this job was that I'd never met the girl who I was to attack and I didn't really feel that comfortable with her.

We rehearsed the scene with how I was to attack her carefully choreographed. I had to bring her to the ground safely, while making it look as if I was hurting her.

I've said already that extras can't act, so I was given ten minutes to pop off and get myself into character.

It was horrible being so mean. Once I got her to the ground, I had to hit her in the head a few times and then attempt to unzip my trousers before she kicked me.

Although very nasty - and made even more so by the fact that this awful experience had happened in real life to a real girl - I was quite proud of how it turned out. Usually when you film something it can be anything from six weeks to eighteen months, before it's transmitted but this was on television two days later.

The director had come up to me after the scene and had very kindly congratulated me on it and warned me that it might be too horrific for evening television viewing, so I should expect it to be cut.

Several other reconstructions were also filmed that day so I didn't expect to see this one on TV. (As I said earlier, never expect anything to be quite as you think it is until it's transmitted).

As it happened it did get transmitted and the weirdest thing was at the end of the reconstruction, they blurred into a photo of the real rapist. I actually though it was fading into a picture of me, as I actually resembled this man rather a lot!

5th October 2005 – Coronation Street

Most episodes of the soaps are pretty much the same. You tend to forget what you did as nothing out of the ordinary stands out. However on this particular day it was my first time in the Rovers Return bar as our Weatherfield Arms was no longer in the show.

Several of us had spent the morning in the Rovers and then at lunch time when everybody else was being signed out, I was asked to stay as there would be new extras in that afternoon.

Everyone went to lunch and I sat there on my own in the male extras' waiting room (we have different extras' rooms if we're working inside the main studio). After munching on my sandwiches, (I refuse to pay for my dinner), I decided to go back to the Rovers to wait for the next scene.

I had thought the AD had said that I was going to be in the Rovers for the first set up after lunch and then I would be wrapped.

Sitting in the big double chair behind the entrance door at the Rovers, I felt a little sleepy. Everyone was on lunch and it was so quiet. I decided to lie down and close my eyes for five minutes.

The next thing I knew, I could hear inside my head "Ken Barlow" shouting to either "Tracy" or "Deirdre" that there was a dead man lying in the lounge? It was so surreal. My first thought was that I was lying at home hearing the TV set.

I came around and realised I had been fast asleep hidden in the Rovers set and they were filming another scene in Ken's house right next to me. It's weird to explain but when you hear those very familiar voices of actors whom you have been watching all your life, it reminds you subconsciously of being safe and sound in your home. Suddenly to become fully conscious and to realise that you're in the bloody studio is just totally weird.

I panicked and thought they had assumed I wasn't around and I was going to get in trouble. I got up and sneaked around the corner quietly so as not to make a noise while they were filming at Ken's house.

I found the AD, who hadn't even noticed that I was missing, so I was sent to sit on a stool with the other new extras at "Roy's Rolls" which was in fact the setting for the scene that I was going to do later on in the afternoon!

7th October 2005 – Doctor Who – New Earth

This extra date was supposed to have been earlier but they had to cancel and reschedule several times until it finally happened.

The four "hero" patients were brought back in to the show but this time we were at the studio, which back then, was based between Newport and Cardiff.

As always I had got there so early that I decided to sleep in the car for a few hours until my call time.

I set my alarm and went to the studio when the time came. I was sent up to costume passing the Dalek from last series' Dalek story at the bottom of the stairs. Cool!

After costume I was sent to make-up with the other three extras (Simon, Melissa and Kirsty), where we spent hours, there being no hurry today.

Whilst in make-up I mentioned that I'd heard that the Cybermen were coming back into the show. Such a shame I said, that I wasn't a bit taller, as I would have loved to have been a Cyberman.

"The Cybermen costumes look amazing," the make-up/prosthetic guys replied. "And the chances are that you're not too small anyway. You're about the same size as Paul Kasey and the costumes are based on his frame. They'll be casting for Cybermen soon."

I made a big enough fuss that day that finally the third AD agreed to put me up for a casting, but I wasn't to say what the casting was for. I couldn't believe it. I was so excited. That would have been the pinnacle of my life as an extra. I know it sounds sad and I had a perfectly good, secure, well regarded and well paid real job so why would I want to be a monster in Doctor Who? It's just one of those things that I had always wanted, to be a monster in a science fiction show, be it Star Wars, Doctor Who or anything. I'd been watching those shows all my life.

Lunch that day was fun as we sat with some shaolin monks who were filming on a different episode, (Tooth and Claw) on the same day.

Finally, we were called for, and we went around the studio and up some stairs to a tiny set that consisted of 2 wooden lifts with lots of water bottles all around them.

Besides our hospital patient nightshirts we also had dressing gowns on to keep us warm as the studio was jolly cold.

The Doctor himself was in the lift, together with us four all going to get a good soaking. Poor Billie Piper had already had her go and now it was our turn and the Doctor's!

We did a rehearsal without water as this could only really be done once, or everyone would be soaking wet.

Then it came to the take. They had asked us to act as if the water were scalding us and to mime screaming. Ah, mime! That's what we do. We are never really talking. It's just our mouths moving pretending to talk as the boom does not want to pick up our voices. We just talk rubbish and nod a bit. Sometimes you can see two people talking at exactly the same time when they mime and sometimes you get the "noddies" who over exaggerate everything with pointing, nodding, and opening their mouths like gold fish!

When you hear what sounds like extras chatting, you are actually hearing something called a wild-track, which is recorded separately and placed onto the scene in the edit, much like a sound effect, the same is done with backing songs.

They called action and we went into the lift, much like we did on the location only this time the camera was facing the other way. The water came on and it was absolutely freezing. We didn't need to fake scream as our faces told the whole story of just how cold that water was.

They cut after what seemed like an eternity and we thought that was it. Nope. They wanted to do it again and although we started off wet, we had to go again straight away.

I was so cold that I stared to turn purple.

They called cut and although it was brilliant fun, (hey, who can say they have had a 'fivesome' in the shower with David Tennant?) I was simply so cold that I had to have the nighty taken off to dry. Right there and then costume took it off me and I was left standing there in front of the actors and crew in just my underwear! But I didn't care at that point and they helped me dry off as soon as possible.

Most of the make-up was off by now but we were told just to leave it until later in case they wanted it touched up for a re shoot. So we got into our real clothes while the costume was dried

I spoke to the first AD and asked if it was possible, now that it had already been on TV and was no longer a secret, for me to have my photograph taken in the TARDIS set. I had to ask but didn't expect him to say...."yes" just so long as I was quick about it.

I took Melissa with me as she was also a Who fan and wanted her photo there too.

We went into the TARDIS set and realised that people were in there, setting up what looked like a lot of clothes racks, which I discovered later were for that scene in The Christmas Invasion where the Tenth Doctor chooses his new costume.

I explained what we were doing and that we had permission and they were fine about it. Apparently all the crew had already done the same thing.

2005 – Doctor who – Cyberman casting

I got a date to go to the casting for an unnamed monster on Doctor Who. In fact, I already knew that it was the Cybermen, as I had made such a big deal of going.

At work I asked my boss the biggest favour ever - the favour to end all favours.

They would be filming for 6 weeks but I only had 4 weeks holiday left, so I asked if I could take all four weeks and have the final fortnight as unpaid leave. He knew just how much it meant to me and agreed, on the condition that all my projects were in by the time the shooting started.

I made one big massive mistake, one that I try not to do anymore; I assumed I would get the role.

Why wouldn't they give it to me? I had already done skin work (work in a costume) and I was the right build, plus I really wanted this more than I'd ever wanted anything.

It's funny now when people take the mickey by asking me, "Were you a Dalek in Doctor Who?" If only they knew what I'd give to be a monster in the show.

Well this was it. I'd worked my socks off to get the casting and I here I was. I was in fact, the first on the list for the day!

I got down to BBC studios in Cardiff and sat in the car for ages as I was stupidly early as usual. I had no idea what the casting would be like but I knew the job was mine.

When it was time to go in, I got to the front reception desk and was told to wait. Three other extras came in to wait as well.

Extra Time

We were introduced to a girl who took us up to meet Alisa Berk. Brilliant! I had met her only recently, on New Earth, so that would be another advantage.

We were still not officially being told what we were casting for, but we all knew.

They played a heartbeat sound to us and told us that we would need to march to this beat in a moment. We were shown a route to take in time with the beat and told we would be nigh on blindfolded.

We were then split into two teams of two and sent away for five minutes to practice with our new partners but it wasn't as easy as it looked.

We were then given "Auton" masks that had been molded around other actors' faces and had to put them on. We couldn't see anything in them. I had to lean right down just to see my feet as the eyes were just pin pricks. So I used my hands to feel if the other chap was in line next to me. The heartbeat started and off we went.

I guess it was not good. I waited all week for the call but it never came. Finally I called the agency and was told that all those who had been picked had been told already.

I was heartbroken. Even now I know a lot of the monster chaps but I still don't get a look in. The agency are still picking new guys but they never call me. I couldn't have been any more subtle what with the e-mail to the agency boss pleading to be a Doctor Who monster.

2005 - Reconstruction Police Bravery awards

I got a call asking, somewhat randomly, if I had ever used a gun before and if I would like to be a shooter in a crime reconstruction for the Police Bravery Awards. How could I turn down such an offer?

I had to go to Rochester one afternoon after work, a little bit of a diversion from my usual route between Bradford and Derby.

As I imagine you are coming to expect by now, I arrived early and sat in the car for an hour or so waiting for all the crew and facilities to turn up. I waited and waited and thought that I must have the wrong address. I got out of the car and started walking about. It turned out that they had set up a tiny base in a park around the back of some houses in a not particularly nice part of town. There were three of us booked and it turned out that my partner in this reconstruction was Monica as usual.

The director introduced himself and we went into the production office to talk. This was weird as I'm not used to being treated like a real person on set. I was told the story of the film and I met with the real policemen that had been involved in the incident. This, I was informed, was the exact place where the shooting had happened

.

I was playing this man who was being chased by a 'friend', in an argument over a girl. We were both to run into an alley, at which point, I would take out a gun and shoot him. The police then would turn up and arrest us both. Then my ex-girlfriend was to turn up, shout a little and also get arrested.

The first few scenes were easy. I was being chased by the other chap. We ran through the streets with him shouting obscenities at me this wasn't difficult but by now it was quite late at night and no one was even bothering to look out of their windows at us. I know the police had told the locals we were coming but you'd still think that they'd have a little gawp!

The next part of the scene was where we nearly had an accident. The plan was for me to run at full speed down an alley and out into the road with other chap running after me, still shouting at me. We both had to cross the road and then a random passing police car would stop.

They promised us that the timing would be okay.

So, "action"! I ran as fast as I could down the alley my pursuer held back a few seconds before pelting down after me with his mouthful of foul language.

I ran and ran, until I got to the road where the camera and a second camera were set up to catch the action.

The police car had arrived too early and was travelling at a good speed along the road. I ran out into the traffic, having been promised that all was safe, without looking and the police car had to skid to a halt as I skimmed past it just in time. We all kept on going and the other chap had to run behind the car.

The poor health and safety guy was so sorry and very pleased that they had captured it on both cameras so we wouldn't be forced to do that shot again.

In the following scene the camera caught up to us while I took the gun out of my pocket and pointed it at the other guy (not an Oscar moment but that's what happens when you hire extras to do actors' jobs)

I got gun training on set again and pointed out that this was the same type of revolver that I'd used a little while ago on "Flyboys".

On the first take, I got the gun out and pointed it shouting something like "Don't get any closer" or some other dumb line that I made up on the spot.

The policemen who had been in the car caught up with us, shouted for me to drop the gun and then ran at me and knocked me to the ground!

The first take must have looked very natural, simply because I had no idea that they were really going to knock me to the ground without any padding at such a force. You see the policemen used in the film were real policemen and not extras!

I had to keep hold of the gun and pretend to drop it while being held on the floor because they didn't want to damage the gun.

I don't think they expected me to drop quite as easily as I did and one of the policemen accidentally banged my face against the pavement.

This would have looked great, I tried to keep in character but he was so distraught that he stopped the filming to see if I was okay, which I would have been, if we'd carried on. Now however, we had to do the entire scene all over again. (We never stop "acting" until we hear the word cut)

On the second take, not having been stunt trained, or even just trained how to fall over safely, I froze. As soon as the policemen shouted at me to stop where I was and to drop the gun, I just seized up and tried to protect myself.

The police men jumped on top of me and pulled my arms behind my back and sat on my elbows! If this is what it's like to be arrested, then it's not a particularly nice experience.

Even shooting the gun didn't bring the locals to their windows although by now it was about two o'clock in the morning!

By the time we had finished the scene, I was bruised all over and aching from head to toe.

A few weeks later, I was on the internet and I looked up the film. It turned out that it had won the Police Bravery Awards for 2005. The award had been presented by the Prime Minister, Tony Blair.

I was so proud, I felt as if I'd won the award, but I soon understood that it was all about the policemen involved and not my amazing acting skills!!

10th January 2006 – AA Commercial

This was a two-day job. I received a call from my brilliant booker in Manchester who told me that he knew it was not going to be a good job but said that he needed a serious amount of people. So, he asked me, would I be willing to go to Manchester for a day for a rehearsal that would last six hours and then from there to go and do the AA commercial. I agreed even though it was for stupidly low money.

The first day I had to park in Manchester and pay for the whole day. We were in a big building and there turned out to be around three hundred of us.

Only about forty of us were from my agency and we all knew each other but we were a little baffled as to what was going on. Everything seemed set up more for a large presentation than for a rehearsal. I had guessed we were all going to get into giant people-sized letters for the advert, or something daft like that.

Finally a young chap came onto stage and introduced himself and told us how excited he was that we had a very important guest today, the director of the advert, who had made big movies (I guess I can't name him here). We were all wondering, "If he's that big, why he is making a UK TV advert?"

We were then given the words to the Carole King song "You've Got a Friend", which was played over and over and over.

We had to learn the words. This seemed silly but we guessed we'd be singing this en masse in the commercial.

Nope. That wasn't the plan. The plan was for all of us, one by one, to sing some of this song solo in front of all three hundred people in that room to see how good we were at singing.

Why didn't they ask us before they booked us? I can't sing for anything. I was born with a love for acting, singing and dancing but not the least bit of talent for any of them.

It was awful, we all had to sing one by one and to make matters worse there was a behind the scenes cameraman filming the whole thing. Great so now we can be seen in-house on the corporate screens in every AA office doing a really bad version of this song.

Extra Time

Thirty or so people were asked to stay in the big hall and the rest of us asked to wait outside on the stairs. It was a bit of a squeeze but we had to wait until we were officially released. We got a call about the filming date a few days later.

On extra jobs in the north, we are not paid as much money as we are down south, so when we're booked on jobs with a lot of people, we get a low rate and they don't have to pay overtime, however many hours we work.

A few days later we had to meet in Manchester Piccadilly Train station at four o'clock in the morning so I had to get up at one o'clock to get dressed and drive to Manchester.

We were taken off in coaches to the Lake District, where we were given jackets and then taken by mini-buses to the location.

 It was so very cold and there was no shelter. It rained all day and all we had to do was walk up and down a hill whilst singing the song!

It got to the point where we were soaked right through to the skin. There was nothing we could do and we kind of became zombies, walking and singing and regretting having ever become TV extras!

Lunch was brought up to location in the back of a car, cold and in little polystyrene containers but due to a miscalculation there wasn't enough for everybody.

Finally we wrapped and got back to the coaches. It was so cold that our teeth were chattering. This was about seven o'clock at night and before the coach left, an AD came in and said that they loved what had been shot today so would we like to come back tomorrow for some of the same thing!

I've never seen so many extras not volunteer for work!

This particular assignment still gets talked about, to this day, as the worst job ever.

5th March 2006 - Vincent

"Vincent" was an ITV drama that starred Ray Winstone, on which we did a lot of days over a long period. I just remember getting to the location with my friend (back in the days when it used to be the same people on every job), who had just worked a night shift as a taxi driver in Halifax before coming straight to this shoot.

When the extras are kept busy, you can get away with being tired and catch up that night but sometimes (most of the time) we're just left waiting all day, doing next to nothing until wrap (which is usually two minutes before overtime).

Well we were left in the same seats and in a nice warm location all day and not used. My friend just slept the whole day away and got paid for the privilege.

During April of that year I got a call from my London agent who asked if I would like to go for a casting for Bad Girls. It was my first casting so I went all the way to London, parked up, got the tube, took out my A-Z, found the building I was looking for, went in and introduced myself and was left to wait... and wait... and wait.

Finally someone came to fetch me and brought me upstairs to meet someone.

I went into this room and stood in front of three people who asked me to give my name, agency and age.

That was it! No questions or acting needed.

I'd driven 110 miles to London and now was driving the 110 miles home. I had cost me a whole day off!

I never heard anything so assumed that I hadn't got the job then one evening, I happened to be out in London with some friends when my telephone rang.

"Hello John, Just to let you know the director really liked you the other day and is considering offering you the role in Bad Girls"

"Okay".

"He'll make a decision within the hour and we'll call you back. If you don't hear anything, assume you've not got it."

Wow. How did that happen?

13th April 2006 – Bad Girls

I was out and about in London with my friends the night before this job, when I got a call quite late asking if I was still interested in the Bad Girls job that I had been cast for a week previously. I said 'yes' and the agency said that they would call me back within the hour as I was now heavily penciled to play Natalie's Boyfriend.

I kept my phone in my hand for about two hours, but there was no call-back, so guessing that I would not be needed, I stayed in London until very late and got back to Derbyshire at 3 in the morning.

It was midday the next day. I was *so* tired, but I was being good and getting on with some work, editing a training film when the telephone rang.

"Hi John, the director decided he likes you and wants you to play Natalie's boyfriend"

"Okay, when and where?"

"Half past five tonight in East Greenwich"

What? Today? Oh my lord. I was unshaven and looked a right mess. I asked the agent what I would be doing and she said that as far as she knew I would be breaking someone out of jail, so best not shave and take scruffy clothes. By the way, there wasn't any parking.

I did as I was told, packed a bag with 'Corrie' clothes and looked up the location on the internet. At this point I had got as far as getting the internet but sat-nav was still some way off! I drew a map of the area and checked it against my A-Z.

I got into the car and drove as fast as I (legally) could down the M1 toward London.

Half way there my phone rang. "Hello this is the Bad Girls costume department," came a voice. "You're Natalie's partner and you've been mentioned in the series before. You're rich so bring a smart suit and be clean shaven."

Panic stricken I explained the situation and she put me at ease, assuring me that they would sort it out when I got there.

I finally found the location, in a pub and there was in fact fairly cheap parking around the corner.

I grabbed my stuff and went into the pub. To my surprise it was business as usual. There was no one who looked as if they might be crew or actors and no TV/film facilities vehicles outside.

I don't usually drink alcohol but I felt I needed one then after rushing down to London in record time, so I sat there with a pint of cider. But was this the right place?

I checked what I had written down and it seemed right but there was still no sign of cast or crew.

Half past five came and went and by now I was really panicking. I couldn't go anywhere in case someone came looking for me to take me to another location but I had my telephone at hand ready for the agency to call and shout at me for making whatever mess up I had!

Finally the crew all turned up rather stressed. The extras' names were called out and it turned out that most of the other drinkers in the pub were also extras!

I was ushered out the back with the costume and make-up departments, who went through my clothes to find something suitable. Everyone was stressing that we were late but I suspected that they were just behind schedule and had been moving from location to location.

Outside the street was cleared of parked cars. I don't know how they did it but they had secured the street and were setting up cameras outside.

I had never watched Bad Girls so had no idea who was in it and whether any of the actors were already there.

They dressed me up in semi-smart clothes, introduced me to the 3rd and the 1st AD and then plonked me on a table right in front of the camera! The other extras were placed at the back of the pub to fill the place up.

Normally I would have been a tad worried by this set up but luckily I'd had a pint of cider, far too much for me as I'm not used to drinking, so my nerves were pretty cool considering what was about to happen.

I was just sitting in my position with the camera guy taking a tape measure to me through the open window to measure the focus and then the sound chap started setting me up with an aerial mike.

"Why are you setting that up?" I innocently ask the sound chap

"So we can hear what you're saying" was his reply

"What I'm saying? What am I saying?" I asked

"Has no one given you the script?"

"Erm... No, I wasn't aware I was saying anything." At that point it dawned on me. All this crew, the closed road, the whole pub, all the extras, everyone was here just for me! Oh my lord!

The sound chap spoke to the 1st and he and the third came over with the script. Most of it was Natalie talking, with me just giving the odd reply, "okay", "sorted", "no problem", that sort of thing. The third was going to read in Natalie's role.

I did it a few times, getting more comfortable each time, twisting a cigarette around in my fingers and talking on the mobile phone but keeping my eyes on the dart board as if I was gazing at nothing in particular and acting slimy! I'm good at that.

There were a few other bits and pieces and it actually made me feel so good inside. I actually felt special for this small moment. It wasn't the first time I'd spoken on TV (I think we used to get lines every time we did Hollyoaks), but it was the fact that I had had no idea that I was going to speak or be the only 'actor' present. I had pulled it off.

I was hoping this could be a nice regular role on Bad Girls, but as it turned out, the character of Natalie was killed off that very episode and the series itself was cancelled shortly afterwards.

17th April 2006 – Enchantment – Times Square Extra

This was my only unofficial job. I was a little naughty while on a trip to New York.

Our hotel was based right around the corner from Times Square and from our window we had been watching the setting up of a big movie all day.

My friends and I were on our way back to the hotel and had to pass through Times Square. It was amazing to see such a large set up. The place was filled with hundreds of extras and crew plus as many cars and taxis (each with a fake movie phone number on the side).

The ADs had shouted at all of the tourists to get back, as the Square was now closed until morning. No one was supposed to be on the square unless they were with the movie.

The movie was called Enchantment and starred Amy Adams (whom I'd not heard of back then) and Susan Sarandon (whom we had spotted in town the night before).

I had never been on anywhere near so big a production. The blocks around the square were all packed with facility vehicles, making it seem as if the whole of New York had been taken over.

When we heard the ADs laying the law down to the tourists I looked at my friend and he knew exactly what was in my mind. I loved being an extra,so I gave him my bag and said that I would see him later. The AD gave me a hard stare and asked if I was with the movie. I nodded, not wanting to speak unless I had to. I have a very English accent and there is no way I could convince anyone that I was American - I can't even convince people at home that I'm from anywhere other than down south!

I found a group of extras in the centre and just stuck by them, (there were hundreds of them).

I tried to mind my own business so that people wouldn't speak to me but unfortunately Americans have a knack for being really friendly! Every time I tried to walk near the edge of the extras in their packs without giving any sort of eye contact, someone would say hello to me. I guessed the Americans were like us and had known each other for a while and were used to seeing the same faces.

I lit a cigarette to give me a better reason to be walking apart from the other extras. I was so worried that as soon as they spoke to me and discovered that I was English, then a whole host of questions would come up, including which agency I was with and where in the States I lived. I know little of such things so it was best to avoid all of them.

The scene featured Amy Adams sitting in a drain right in the middle of Times Square with a big lorry whizzing past her!

Before long, one of the many ADs came over saying "I need ten people." He then promptly indicated ten random people. "1, 2, 3, 4, 5, 6, 7, 8, 9" and then pointed at me with the word "ten!"

"Right, you guys are going to walk in front of this cab while it waits for the walk sign" and then he pointed at me again and said "You can walk behind the cab once it's stationary."

I felt I was being singled out. Perhaps he knew I was a fake! There were hundreds of extras that day and our small part in the background isn't even noticeable.

The worst part was when he said "I need all your numbers" I had never worked with numbers back then as we'd always been names on UK sets (I have since learnt that numbers are sometimes used in the UK too.)

I listened as the other nine extras gave their numbers "135", "120", "90", "75" and so on. The AD wrote them down and then said "I only have nine, who have I missed?"

This was it. Why had I decided to be an extra in the US? I just wanted to vanish, but there were thousands of people all from the film in the square. It felt like that scene in the film Invasion of the Body Snatchers when the good guys give away that they have feelings...

I put my hand up.

"What's your number?"

I put on my best American accent and picked a random number similar to those used and hoped that someone else standing there wouldn't be that number and said "124"

No funny looks, no shouts, no reveal! I had got away with it.

We did the scene many times. I think before long everyone decided that I wasn't the friendly type and left me alone to do my little walk behind the taxi.

Around one o'clock in the morning they must have called for lunch as suddenly Times Square just emptied and loads of extras all walked in a long queue around the block. I followed but when I realised I'd be cornered inside a building for lunch, I decided just to go back to the hotel to bed!

7th June 2006 – New Street Law - Lawyer

Our Manchester agency had a new booking agent called Charlie whom I loved. He'd come from Red Productions and I hope he's still in the industry somewhere today. What makes a great booking agent is knowing what you look like, what your character is like and how well you can deal with lines if need be and of course how reliable you are. Charlie was brilliant.

On this day Charlie had booked us to do "New Street Law". Our agency had the monopoly on this show, which I guess was something to do with Charlie, as it was made by Red Productions.

This was a show about lawyers, (the clue is in the title), and we were asked to bring suits and smart casual wear. My favourite! No 'Corrie' clothes for me today.

There were about thirty of us booked, all from our agency and we took it in turns to go to costume to check what we had with us.

Extra Time

The rumour was going around that lots of people had not brought suits with them and were being sent home.

It was true. There must have been twenty people who turned up without suits. Now, extras are not important in the grand scheme of things, as I said earlier, we are just breathing props that eat all the food and complain a lot, but when lots of extras make a mistake like this, it can cost a production a lot of money as the shoot cannot go ahead as planned.

The 2nd AD was on the phone to the agency in minutes and a call went out to all other Manchester-based extras agencies with the message that all extras had to be suited and ready on set as soon as humanly possible.

I guess the other agencies couldn't believe their luck as this was their chance to slip into this production, which still had a good few months shooting to go, (although the season was actually cut back in the end and then ultimately cancelled.)

Charlie called me up "John, who didn't bring their suits with them today from our agency?" Oh my lord he wanted me to snitch on the other extras. I didn't have many friends as it was, without blabbing their names out.

"Just check to see who got signed out at eight thirty and who didn't. Those of us who are still here are the ones who brought all the correct costume."

I know Charlie came down to see the production office in person to apologise but I have no idea of the outcome, as I never did that show again. This was a pity as it was a nice show to do. I always judge whether an actor is a nice person or not by their attitude to us extras. If they at least acknowledge that we exist, then they're OK by me. Just a nod will do. John Hannah, the star of New Street Law, was fantastic and spoke to everyone.

This pleased me, as I had liked him in the Mummy movies. I hate it when I have admired someone who then turns out to be less than friendly and doesn't even give you eye contact. I was ready to name some names then but let's stay positive. In any case, just because I have taken a dislike to someone, it doesn't necessarily mean that he or she is not a nice person. There! Positive and balanced!

28th June 2006 – Made of Honor (one of the regulars in a Scottish Pub)

My London agency had contacted me about a film called "Made of Honour" asking if I would be available for a day on location. I had still done very few films, so was very excited at the prospect.

I left my home in Derbyshire super early as always but for the life of me could not find the location, which was a village not far from London. This was still before sat-nav so I used the UK map I carried in the car and drove around the area where I knew it was for ages. Even these days, sat-navs are great for finding towns but I never rely solely on one to find TV locations as they are often found up some track or unnamed road that no one has told the sat-nav about. Sometimes even the postcode gets you to the wrong town!

For first time I was nearly late. OK, so I was still the first extra there out of about 100 of us and I beat most of the crew but I wasn't the full hour early that I always had been up to now.

The pub we were filming in was supposed to be in Scotland somewhere so I got to wear the sort of clothes that I don't usually wear on TV. At the request of the costume department, I'd even gone out and bought a chequered shirt, which I've never worn since.

There were several scenes in the pub but it was one of those days when I wasn't really needed. I spent most of the day sitting outside in the sun. It was such a quaint village and it seemed wrong that the adjacent field was filled up with our lot. When a film comes to town, people know it. There are trucks, buses, catering vehicles, mobile toilets and trailers, not to mention everybody's cars.

10th July 2006 – Hollyoaks in the City – Slimy Heckler

I really enjoyed working on this show. I was never a Hollyoaks fan but I did a good few days on "Hollyoaks; In the City" and really enjoyed it. They'd spent some money on good production values and great directors.

Initially I had been asked if I fancied playing a 'cottager'. I had just assumed that that meant someone who owned a cottage. It was a speaking role, but I was unable to take the time off work, so I got a much smaller part instead. It was a night-shoot so I didn't have to get any time off work. I was one of a bunch of guys waiting to see a strip show but ending up seeing a singing transvestite instead. I had to shout "get off ," or something similar.

I'm only telling this story as a reminder that it doesn't matter what you film or what you do in a shot, it still does not mean that it'll make it onto television. This scene was totally cut out! I was pleased to get the role as "Slimy Heckler" but upset that it wasn't in the final cut as I loved this show. If only they would release this short-lived series on DVD.

This may have been the first time that a speaking role of mine was cut but it certainly wasn't the last. An extra is never important, even if he has been given a speaking role. Even when you do get a line or two, you usually only get one shot at it; after all if it were important then they would have hired an actor.

Tuesday 31st August/Friday 1st September 2006

Trial and Retribution – In The Public Gallery

I think this was the first time that I worked at Kingston-upon-Thames Courthouse. This has to be one of the most used locations on British television, not just for the court interiors, the exterior makes a good Buckingham Palace too.

This was another case of a not particularly exciting scene or memorable experience. It was however, the day when I was sitting on the bus, somewhere in the middle, with what appeared to be a group of new extras behind me, and a bunch of old hands at the front. The guys at the back were really excited about doing some TV work but the ones at the front wanted nothing to do with them, as they were seasoned extras.

This was the day I learnt a new word. That word is S.A.

The trouble with being an extra is that all you need to be able to do is breath and walk. Scrub that, you don't even need to be able to walk. As long as you are alive then you're already as well qualified as you'll ever need to be, to be an extra!

Just turn up to work and do as you're told. It really is that simple. Unfortunately some people have a problem with the fact that no experience is needed, you need know nothing about film making and you're only there as a breathing prop.

You're not actually involved in the making of the production; you are part of the finished picture, the movement in the background. The job is so demeaning that out-of-work actors are advised to get a job in a fast food retail chain rather than be an extra.

I'm not slagging the job off as I absolutely love it. It's brilliant but it does turn your brain to jelly and can play havoc with your self-worth.

Some extras having developed a problem with this over time, want to feel important. So they have invented a special term that only extras know - *Supporting Artiste*.

I've been on set before and seen extras rip down the message on the bus that says "Extras holding bus" as they're so insulted at being referred to as 'extras'. The fact that only extras call themselves *SA's* is beside the point. No one outside the world of the extra knows what an *SA* is!

It's all kind of weird, but unfortunately as I have said many times before, this is the only job in the world that you never move up in. It doesn't matter if you're an extra for one job or for forty years, you'll still be just an extra.

I was still living in Derbyshire at this time and didn't do much London work. The guys at the front of the bus had pretty much ignored me most of the day, assuming, I imagine, that I was a new extra. I started chatting to them and they seemed to be quite impressed that I'd had so many speaking roles. I guessed that they were not as easy to get down south as they were in the north. Anyway, this seemed to impress them enough for them to invite me to the front of the bus.

When one of them asked me if I did anything besides "SA" work I replied that I headed up the internal corporate film department for Morrison's and wrote, cast, edited and so on films for over 150,000 people within the firm. "I'm based at home in Derbyshire but have an area in the Bradford Head Office."

This piqued their curiosity and one of them asked me why I did "SA work". I replied, "Because I enjoy it, it's a bit of fun"

They went mad at me. "Fun? This isn't fun. This is people's livelihoods and you're taking work away from people who need it!"

"This isn't work" I objected," no one could possibly do this for a living"! How wrong I turned out to be but that story is for later on.

The other thing I really remember about one of these days is being outside the building looking at the Second World War bullet holes in the wall and having a cigarette when the Set Medic came up to me.

I said hello but he suddenly laid into me about smoking. if I had seen the things he'd seen then I wouldn't do it. If I ever got ill from smoking then there would be no way in hell that he would lift a finger to look after me.

He just went mad at me and went on and on. It wasn't like I was even close to him so he'd come over the car park just to say these things to me.

Friday 8th September 2006 – Doctor Who: The Shakespeare Code - Trumpeter

I was up in Bradford filming a really exciting all day pharmacy conference for work when around teatime I got a call from my agent. Would I be free for Doctor Who the following day, and would I mind shaving off my goatee beard again. My boss was standing right next to me, so I asked him (begged might be a more accurate word) and he agreed to my going, so long as I made up the missing day at the weekend.

I went home and shaved off my beard as usual, very excited to be returning to Doctor Who.

As you know, I'm always early to every set but with anything Doctor Who related I make a special point of it.

I got up ridiculously early and drove all the way from Derbyshire to the Treforrest Industrial Estate at Pontypridd, not too far from Cardiff, singing along with the stereo as I drove, so excited to be a part of another Doctor Who episode. The drive went well, with no traffic but to be fair this was stupid o'clock in the morning and I didn't expect any issues.

The problem was that when I arrived at the industrial estate, I couldn't find the estate!

I looked everywhere. I drove to every building up and down the road over and over again. I stopped at the estate map and examined it the best I could. The map was on a sign about eight feet in the air that I doubt even lorry drivers could actually see!

I just drove and drove, round and round and then I saw someone. He looked like an extra. My god I can spot extras in the real world now. I stopped and asked him if he was and sure enough YES - and he knew the way. I would never have found it without him.

When I arrived, I was sent to costume last. There were other extras there, but they'd been there the previous day, so I was not needed yet.

I was booked as a trumpeter and I knew they had filmed in the Globe Theatre in London so I kind of guessed what my costume would look like.

I was told that someone had already been booked as the trumpeter in London on location at the Globe but it was decided that they would do this particular scene back in the studio so he was never used.

I didn't mind having to wear tights, as that's all part of the job, but what I didn't expect was the nappy style codpiece that was sewn in from the back to stop it from falling off.

I'd spent the morning drinking coffee while waiting to go into costume and it didn't cross my mind that I would be wearing something that didn't account for toilet breaks.

I ended up only going to the toilet once that day (It must have been quite an experience for me to actually remember my toilet break) and it didn't prove easy. Coffee and drinks in general were off the menu for me for the rest of the day.

Having shaved my beard off the night before, I was surprised that costume then decided that I would look good with a goatee beard (granted it was bigger than mine).

I strolled around the base a little and got chatting to two lovely ladies, Amanda Lawrence and Linda Clark, both of whom were dressed in full costume and make-up as witches. The make-up was amazing. I went right up to them to have a look and you simply couldn't tell it wasn't real.

Extra Time

I also got to have a chat to Dean Lennox Kelly about the series 'Sorted' that I had met him on and enjoyed watching, and about his leaving 'Shameless'.

Everyone was so nice, but when they were all on set I waited in the rickety old extras bus as the other extras came and went until finally, after lunch I was called onto set. Unfortunately even though I had seen David Tennant and Freema Agyeman walking about all day, in and out the studio, they were not in my scene. I was dying to meet Freema, who was playing the new companion Martha Jones, to find out what she was like. (Would she pass the 'acknowledge an extra' test?)

The set was simply a reproduction of the stage from the Globe Theatre. I was given a place to stand and Props gave me a trumpet. It hadn't crossed my mind that I was expected to play it. (No, I do not have trumpet playing on my list of Extras' skills)

As I stood there, the camera team set up tracks and a dolly (little train tracks for the camera, the dolly being a device to lift the camera up and down smoothly); and Phil Collinson, the producer of Doctor Who came up to me and told me to lift the trumpet as the camera passes and just play anything.

Play anything?

I told him I couldn't play. "They've sent you an extra to play trumpet, who doesn't play the trumpet!"

To this day I don't know if he already I knew I wouldn't be able to play.

It took three goes for me to lift the trumpet at exactly the right height at exactly the right time. (That's about as difficult as it gets being an extra).

I pretended to play and just blew into the trumpet as the camera wiped. That was all there was too it. When I signed out, the 2nd AD said he would get me back soon. I never know whether or not to believe this sort of thing, as there are so many of us and I guess I'm easily forgotten.

The best part about doing Doctor Who is that it's pretty much the only show that I always make a point of watching. So when they pay me for it, I make sure the money is used for my TV licence and on buying the Doctor Who DVD box set, thus making my Doctor Who watching experience even better because it's free!

I don't tend to tell anyone when I'm going to be on TV, as no one is supposed to spot the extras and you never know if you're in shot or not. The reason an extra is called an extra is because we're not supposed to be noticed really. As I keep saying we are just breathing props in the background. Anyway I happened to be at my best friend's house when this episode was broadcast. I hadn't even told him that I had been doing Doctor Who this series, let alone this actual episode. So, we sat and watched and as he's also a geek, he recorded it so we could watch it again.

We watched and my part came on, a really nice slow wipe as the trumpet is heard across London and then, there I was, in full frame.

He said nothing! "He can't have not seen it," I thought. "He's just winding me up because I hadn't told him that I was going to be in it."

The show finished and I couldn't hold back any longer. So I asked, "Did you see me?"

NO! He had no idea and even when I pointed my bit out to him, he refused to believe it was me!

It was only months later when the Doctor Who Magazine Series Three Special was released with a big picture of me on the Shakespeare Code page, that he finally began to believe it was me. Later on a 'Battles In Time' trading card was released featuring my character ('Shakespearean Actor'), so he just had finally to accept the truth.

Tuesday 12th September 2006

Heartbeat – Give Peace a Chance- Slimy Reporter

I got a call to say that I had been picked for a speaking role in Heartbeat. Everyone makes fun of my attempts at accents, so I didn't even try to do a northern one, (remember I only just about got away with saying one number in that rubbish American accent of mine on the set of 'Enchantment'). They sent me the script in the mail which is unusual for an extra.

My bit was so tiny and unimportant. "Just right for the local rag", I had to say in a slimy reporter kind of way. By now I was beginning to notice that the only speaking roles I ever got had the words 'slimy' or 'mean' in the character description, but anyway, they're usually the fun things to play. I have no problem being funny-looking with a large forehead and slitty little eyes if that's what gets me featured parts.

This was one of those sets where every member of the crew was really fantastic and didn't talk to us like shit. I got to go to location in a nice car while the other guys were in a big bus. I never heard the end of them taking the mickey, but the great thing about seeing the same old guys on set is that at some point we all get to have a nice role. It's almost like taking it in turns.

I had no problem back then with what people thought of extras, as I had a really nice job, with a nice company car and probably got paid better than most of the people on set. However, it was still really nice when a crew treated you well, like you mattered.

This was one of the few shows that allowed us to take photos all day, as long as we didn't do it during a take.

My first scene was driving past actor John Duttine (who had starred in the classic sci-fi serial 'The Day of the Triffids') in the rather nice 1960's car that I had been given, and then showing him my press pass. John then just had to look at me and say contemptuously, "That's all we need".

I hadn't got much else to do, so I sat there in the sun all day, watching the filming with one of the guys who was playing a photographer. This was one of the few shows that let passers-by stop and watch and meet the actors and even have some tea and biscuits. They were just such a lovely crew.

Finally my big scene arrived. Remember what I have said about speaking extras? Even these are unimportant. That's why they left me last, right to the end of the day, by which time the light was fading fast. I had learnt my one line and had practised it for the last twenty-four hours. I had to be word perfect and I wasn't going to mess this up.

The director then said to me and the non-speaking photographer "You guys can say whatever you want just so long as it fits in the scene!"

What?

Why go to all the effort of writing a script and sending it to me, only for my line to be so unimportant that I can say anything I liked? I wasn't having this and I said to the director "No, my line is, 'This'll look right on the front of the local rag, (pause) hey?'"

I shouldn't really have said it but he wasn't in the mood to argue as light was going fast. So the photographer and I walked to the car and I leant over the window to say my line. "This'll look right on the front of the local rag"(Pause). Before I could get out my really well practised "Hey?", with a nice snarl at the edge of my lip, the photographer extra took his opportunity to throw some lines in "All-right mate, look up!" What? When did he suddenly get lines? (Why am I still bitter so many years later?)

It was a one take wonder and we were wrapped.

I saw the episode on TV and to show how unimportant extras really are, they used different extras to play our parts in a later scene, plus they took my line and placed it over a different shot of me, even though my lips weren't moving. At least I wasn't dubbed.

Friday 21st September 2006 –

Clothes Conditioner Commercial

I won't use the name of the fabric conditioner advert here but this was just one of those days when you had to throw any dignity or self-respect out of the window.

There weren't many of us in this commercial, which was filmed on a trading estate. In the first shot, a few of us had to go around the aisles of a supermarket with just our pants on and a duvet on our shoulders! To make matters worse, the supermarket was open at the time with just our aisle locked off for filming. At least the costume department did give us new boxer shorts, to go over the top of our own underwear. (I'm at that age now that I get very excited by free socks or pants).

We did the shot, but no one thought to tell us that we could get dressed, while the crew got on with the next shot. It was weird how after a while, I just didn't care what I looked like, as if walking around in pants and a duvet was perfectly normal.

We were told that at our final location of the day we would have a very special guest on set and that we would have to sign disclaimers to say that we wouldn't talk to the press about who it was. We were quite excited by this and many names were mentioned as we speculated as to who our guest might be.

In the North, when commercials break for lunch, the extras aren't allowed to eat the food that is on set. We are paid an extra £5 to buy our own lunch, (this money arrives, together with our wages four months later). This time however, as there were only six of us, and there were no fast food places nearby, we thought that we would be looked after a bit better. We hoped so anyway.

We watched hopefully as the caterers put food platter after food platter onto the crew bus, but still no one had said anything. Finally, we thought we'd be brave and ask if we could have lunch.

"Are you extras?"

"Yes."

"Sorry, we've been told not to feed you. There's not enough for you"

I could have understood this on a day when there were sixty of us, but six? Furthermore, the amount of food being served up for the small crew was just silly.

The previous year I'd done a 'Cleaner Close' commercial, when the director couldn't believe that the extras weren't going to be fed, and had told the caterers to make food for all of us - and there were quite a lot of us on that one.

After lunch the caterers kindly said that we could have the left-overs. We declined. Even we extras with no dignity left didn't want to give them the pleasure of seeing us eat the scraps.

In the afternoon we went to a busy location in Manchester and the "special guest" arrived - an ex EastEnders actress with an entourage of six people or so. We were very disappointed. The best part was that the 'pap' who came out and photographed her all the way from her car to the shop where we were filming, wasn't even a real 'pap', just another extra paid to look like a 'pap'. Weird or what?. He was obviously only paid to take photos as she went in, because when we wrapped, she walked out and down the road without anybody taking the blindest bit of notice of her.

I should have said though, that despite all that, she was really nice to the extras!

Tuesday 3rd Oct 2006 – Torchwood

Random Shoes – Paul Chequer's Body Double

In 2006 I was still working full time at Morrison's making internal training films but my boss was amazing and trusting and if I asked for a day off for Background work, he usually said yes. Boy do I miss that Job…

Okay, so Torchwood, body double.

I remember getting the call from my agent and being quite excited. She had said that I was the same size as the actor Paul Chequer and would be his double. I had just met Paul a few weeks earlier on the set of 'Synchronicity' in Rochdale. (Of course when I say 'met' what I really mean is I saw him and had to move out his way in a scene!)
They didn't tell me anything else. Would I meet Paul or any of the cast from Torchwood? What should I wear? Do I wear his clothes? Nothing!
When I'm not told what to wear or I know it's going to be costume clothes I always put my best pants on just in case. There's nothing worse than having three or four costume girls dressing you while you're standing there in old pants!!!!!
I got onto base, still with no idea what I was in for. There were some other extras there, who were all aware that they were going to be extras in a café. All I knew was that I was going to be Paul Chequer's double, although on this occasion I wasn't actually going to meet him or the director.

The costume department popped by to see all the background artists, checking everybody's clothes and making them change if necessary. It's a ritual that we have to go through on set everyday. This is why being in costume dramas, body doubling or standing in are good jobs to do, as we don't have to carry half our own wardrobe around with us!

Anyway, costume came up to me and said that they wouldn't need to check my costume as I was a stunt man and could change in the costume truck! "Stunt man?" I laughed "No, body double". They didn't laugh. A little worry entered my brain.

In costume, I changed into a copy of Paul's outfit and then was promptly sent to make-up for checks.
Make-up were in two minds whether to wig me or to cut my hair. Finally they decided on a cut, which was nice as it meant a little extra money plus a free haircut. "After all," they laughed, "we don't want a wig to fall off during the stunt!!"
"What stunt?"
"When you get punched!."

"You do know I'm a body double and not a stuntman?"
The girls turned to their boss, who checked the call sheet
"John R Walker right?"
"Yes."
"Well, you're the only person in today to double for the actor and the only doubling needed is a stunt in which you fall onto the ground after being punched."
At this I kept quiet. She must have been right. I must have been hired as a stuntman by mistake. Hey-ho! After all this was Torchwood, part of the legend that is Doctor Who, and if I had to be punched to the ground and pretend to be a stuntman, just to stay in the show, then so be it. How hard

could it be just to fall over and pretend to be hit?

At this point I really had accepted my fate and I didn't want to mess up the whole production by pointing out that I was not, in fact, actually a stuntman, thus throwing the schedule out and probably never being asked back onto the show.

After I had been made up I went back onto the bus with my fellow extras, having decided not to tell them anything. I was now starting to think like a stuntman. I wasn't going to let them or anyone else know that I wasn't one! A lady with an American accent came onto the bus and called my name. I put my hand up and followed her to her production office. I can't remember her name or position and in fact, I never saw her again but whoever she was, on the way to the office she started to tell me the entire plot of the story. However, at that point I was not really listening; I was just waiting to hear about my role in the episode. I mean, it had to be a pretty tough punch if the actor needed a stuntman to do the fall for him!

She went into her tiny office while I stood outside as she looked through her many cupboards, looking for the sign-off sheets for me. I was expecting special 'stunt chits' with insurance stuff and the like on them, rather than the usual BBC chits.

I don't remember her saying anything about my role, as I stood watching her search up and down her cabin for the pad of sheets. The longer it took her to find them, the more I was convinced that they would be something out of the ordinary. They had to be extra-special ones that were not used very often, as the regular Extras chits that she used every day that would be easy to find.

Finally she found a new pad of sheets, placed it on her desk and started to write on the cover slowly and carefully. Why would she make me wait like this? What the hell kind of form was I being asked to fill out here? Then, just as she seemed to be finished writing on the cover she reached for a big green highlighter pen and marked something on the cover. I stood transfixed, awaiting my doom. What kind of stunt insurance, complicated, scary form was I going to have to fill out?

Finally, she filled the first one in and passed it to me to sign!

It was just a normal 'background chit' and not a stunt form at all. I climbed up into her office and signed my name (which, incidentally you should never do at the start of a day), and saw all she had done was to get a new pad of chit forms out and filled in the cover with the pen, making it look pretty with the green highlighter!

My fears subsided. This lady knew that I wasn't a stuntman or she wouldn't have given me a normal chit.

Extras are never told anything. We have to try and learn what we can from snippets of information flying about, (with the exception of Shameless and Holby City, on which we get our own set of sides and call sheets) and usually that information is wrong.

Extras must learn from early on, that we are not part of the film making process. We are not actors or crew but simply props that breathe and need to be placed. So, why should we be told what's going on?

Right, there I was, in costume with my make-up done, when I was rushed onto set with the first of the crew. On the way there I met the 1st AD Nael Abbas. We got chatting and of course, it became clear what a geek I was, so I asked him if he had worked on any other Science Fiction shows, in particular if he had ever worked on my favourite, the Highlander franchise.

It turned out that he was 3rd AD on the 2nd Unit for Highlander 3.

Now, I *love* Highlander. I'd been taking screen grabs from the movie, and I wanted to know who was who on them and what parts were actually shot in Scotland or abroad. I just had so much to ask him. He told me that his team had shot the title sequence of the film, but had never received the recognition that they deserved.

He had also worked on Lexx, which I had loved, and on a show called Star Hunter, which I had never heard of.

"Oh you must see it." he exclaimed so I went home that night and ordered the DVDs of both series. It turned out to be a real hidden gem.

So there I was on the bus getting totally sucked in by a man with whom I could have chatted for days, given the chance, but before I knew it we were on set.

The set was an Indian Restaurant that had been a Little Chef. The Torchwood crew had transformed it back into a typical roadside café. They did their job so well that at least five cars stopped during the course of the day, expecting to find a real restaurant, before security explained to them that it was just a film set.

When we arrived, I was then asked to wait outside until I was needed. I still had no idea what I was doing. Was I to double the fall? There was a big blue crash mat outside and it wasn't a cold day for October so I decided to sit on it and maybe get used to it ready for my stunt.

I waited patiently, as extras do, then drank some coffee; then waited a bit more; then there was some more waiting… All this time, the actors and the main crew were inside working. The other extras turned up and a few at a time, they were called inside. So much for getting me to set first. I sat,

I waited and I drank some more coffee, I waited, I started to drift in and out of consciousness on the blue crash matt. Before long it was lunch time. They took us back down the road for lunch and then brought us back. By now, the big soft blue crash matt had vanished. It must have been taken inside, which not only meant that my big moment of truth was nearly upon me but also that I now didn't have the soft big blue matt to lie on... not that I felt like sleeping any more, as my stomach turned over in fear of what I was going to have to do.

I sat on the mini bus with the spare extras... I waited and waited, and waited and waited, until finally the 3rd AD came out and called my name. "This is it!" I thought.

"John" he said "You've been wrapped"

That was indeed 'it'. The mini bus took me back to base; I changed, signed out and drove the hundred and fifty miles home without actually having been in front of the camera once!!!

Sunday 15th Oct 2006 –

Torchwood - Paul Chequer's Body Double.

I loved this job so much. First of all Torchwood was a spin off from Doctor Who and secondly I was given my own trailer. This does not happen very often to us extras, so when it does we usually sit alone taking photos of ourselves in the trailer until we start to get bored and to miss the other extras. There's always a big sense of pride when you have a trailer of your own but on the other hand, it's not much fun without having other people to tell all about it. It's not unusual for extras in this position to decide to sit in the old bus with the other extras!

I think this was my first time at Treforrest Base as my previous Doctor Who episode had been filmed at the old base. So, when I arrived, I made my way to the Production Office to sign in and was told to wait in the trailer until someone from make-up came to fetch me.

 It was one of those days when there were no other extras on set at all and I was already feeling a bit special, (extras like feeling special).

When I was finally called to costume there was a shock waiting for me. I was going to be a dead body and would be required to wear nothing! I wanted to ask just how 'nothing' nothing was, as I'd heard that this new adult Doctor Who spin-off show would have sex, nudity and swearing in it and I didn't really want to be shoved on set with nothing on at all. As it happens I was allowed to keep my pants on, (thank goodness), and they gave me a massive dressing gown to wear over them. Plus I kept my trainers on for walking around the set.

As I stepped off the costume truck I was asked to go to make-up, where I found myself sitting in my pants and dressing gown next to John Barrowman! He said hello and introduced himself.

"Hi, I'm John".

Nervously I introduced myself, using pretty much the same words as he had, then felt that I had to say something else, just to show how completely at ease I was...

They had recently begun a massive advertising campaign for Torchwood, so I asked John, "How does it feel being on the sides of buses?" I don't remember his answer, just this nonsense coming out of my mouth and thinking what an idiot I was! Over the course of the next few days of the shoot, with two Johns on set (Barrowman and me), I became known to everyone as 'John the Double'.

So anyway, make-up were not sure what to do as I was playing both the dead Paul Chequer and the live version. So they stripped the dressing gown down to my waist and made-up my chest to look dead and tried a wig on me. However, this turned out to look rubbish, so they cut my hair instead.

I asked after Nael Abbas and that crazy American lady who had liked telling everyone more than we ever needed to know, but it turned out that Nael had got another job and to this day I have never seen him again. No one seemed to know who the American lady had been!

I was sent back to wait in my trailer, where I spent the time watching props and costumes being moved around and trying unsuccessfully to get a sneak peek into the open doors of sound stages, until finally a runner came in, calling for me as if I were really late and had just turned up. He was screaming for me to get on set as soon as possible, and I could hear the 1st AD screaming at him to get me on set as soon as possible so we ran!!! I followed him past the TARDIS set, standing there all dark and cold as if dead; to another set where I was waved urgently through the door.

It was like walking into another world. There were so many things to see and look at, but no time to take it all in. Everyone was calling me. "John, can you get onto the slab please?" Before I knew it costume had removed my shoes and my dressing gown, and as if I were not nervous and embarrassed enough, I heard the very familiar voice of John Barrowman coming towards me, shouting, "We have a naked man on set."

Someone ushered me onto the table warning me just in time that it was very cold steel. A cover was placed over my lower half and I was told to play dead for the rehearsal. Action!!!!!

This was the scene where Paul's character Eugene faints upon after seeing his own dead body then gets up again. The shot was super close up on my chest which was supposed to be dead. The trouble was after all that running and with my nerves all shot up I was shaking and breathing really fast. Only minutes before I had been sitting comfortably in the trailer and now I was on set, seeing the Torchwood Hub for the first time and rehearsing a scene in which I was supposed to be dead.

Once the rehearsal was done I finally got to meet Paul Chequer and the director James Erskine who both introduced themselves. James then asked if we could do the scene for a take, but this time would it be possible for me to actually stop breathing so hard! I explained the situation and managed to calm down so they could do the take.

I have been dead a few times now and I find it one the hardest things to do, as you either have to stop breathing altogether or to slow it down so as not to let your stomach muscles being seen moving. I'm a stop breathing person myself. I breathe in, let it out, and then breathe in and let it half out. This has to be done and ready by the time they're clapping the take. It's no good going too early as a take can have started up to thirty seconds before action is called.

Everyone is called to first positions (the starting point of the take). Checks are then done by costume and make-up and any other department who need to make any final adjustments to what will be in the frame. The 1st Assistant Director (1st AD) will then shout for the cameras and sound to turn over and only when both departments have called back to confirm that they are indeed turning and at speed then the clapper person will mark the take for the editor! This is the mid-point of holding breath and with luck the first AD will call action straight after that.

I remember holding my breath and just feeling this massive vein in my neck throbbing like there was no tomorrow. I was so worried that the camera would see it and that James would shout at me, but I think that was more in my mind than anything else.

I've seen that episode of Torchwood on Blu-Ray and during that very scene James and Paul mentioned me in the director's commentary. Nice! Later I was able to thank James when he came up to direct some Waterloo Road episodes.

Anyway, once I had got that scene out of the way things were a lot easier.

I was then introduced (still in my pants) to Eve Myles and Burn Gorman. Standing in my pants to meet actors has since become the norm for me!

The next scene had Eve and Burn discussing whether she, Gwen Cooper, (Eve's character) was going to perform the autopsy on me as she had never done one before. None of this was making sense to me as I lay there, as the show had not yet been on TV!

This was the first time I met Eve. She is so lovely and down to Earth, and puts everyone around at their ease. Although having said that, she did have a (pretend?) argument with props about whether the scalpel she was going to use to cut me open was the fake blunt one or the real sharp one!! To this day I don't know if they were joking!

I did some more dead scenes while Paul was acting his heart out, and then before I knew it, it was lunch time and I was sent to Captain Jack's office to get dressed. This was the first time I saw the set. There was so much to see. Little bits and bobs all over the place and I remember seeing the hand in the jar, but not twigging that it was the Doctor's hand that had been cut off in the fight with the Sycorax in The Christmas Invasion.

Everyone ran to lunch leaving me pretty much to do my own thing. As always I knew there was no need to hurry to lunch as even though I was the only extra I still knew my place and would have to remain until the end of the queue.

I wanted to have a proper look round and managed to catch a props guy before he ran to lunch. He explained to me how tough it was to find pumps for the water towers that were quiet enough not to disturb the filming. I know this seems like pointless information but I'm a geek and need to know such little things!

After lunch I was not needed for a while and feeling more secure and brave, I ventured out of the bus and pottered around a bit until I found myself on the TARDIS console room set.

I took the opportunity to really examine the place; to touch all the buttons, pull every lever, look underneath everything, hell why not? No one was there to tell me not to, as they were all working on set.

Then I saw a piece of paper on the floor under the TARDIS seat. At first I ignored it and carried on playing with the console, realising just how much everyday stuff was in there. Then I looked again at this piece of paper and curiosity took over. I bent down to pick it up. It was a folded £10 note, which must have fallen out of somebody's pocket at some time and was just lying there on the floor under the Doctor's control seat. I picked it up and looked around guiltily, examining the ceiling of the TARDIS set to see if there were any cameras about and whether this was a "You've Been Framed"-style set-up. (I have no idea why I thought these things. I'll put it down to guilt for what I did next).

I couldn't believe my luck, a nice crisp £10 note just lying on the floor, in the TARDIS of all places. Yes, I kept it, but I had nowhere to put it. So, I kept it in my hand under the long sleeves of my dressing gown, and then the runner came looking for me again to take me around the corner back onto the Torchwood Hub set.

I was asked to undress again, so I stuck the £10 note into my shoe! I actually shoved it right the way down. Owning up to it now does not redeem me in any way!

So, I did one more 'dead' scene before going back to costume and make-up and suddenly I was in another set of clothes, just like Paul's except that costume had spent fifteen minutes cutting, scratching and ripping them until I looked like I had been in an accident.

I was sent back on set and this time it was Paul's turn to undress and play dead on the freezing cold stainless steel slab, while I played the back of his head looking at him, (to establish to the audience that he and I were the same person.)

Monday 16th October 2006 –

Torchwood – Paul Chequer's Body Double

The following day I drove back down from Derbyshire again and went straight to Base. I was already feeling a little more confident about this job.

The highlight of my day was sitting in the Costume truck next to John Barrowman and Eve Myles when the Scissor Sisters' song 'I Don't Feel Like Dancin'' came on the radio. John B jumped out of his seat, proclaiming this to be one of the songs that he had been practising for panto in Cardiff, as he danced and sang with the amazing make-up girl. The truck was moving backwards and forwards while they danced and we simply had to sit and watch as no one could do any work with so much movement going on.

As quickly as it started, the song finished and John sat back down into his chair for his make-up to be finished. Brilliant

We were at a new location that day and I hadn't got my trailer any more so it was back to the scruffy old bus for me!

All I did all day was sit on the bus with Eve Myles' double. So much for being needed!

I did get to meet a third Eugene (the part that Paul Chequer and I were playing.) He was the stunt Eugene who did the actual car crash. I felt a little like he'd butted into my job! I was the only Eugene double in this show!

After a whole day of sitting on the bus reading, both the Gwen double and I were wrapped and asked to come back the next day.

Tuesday 17th Oct 2006 –

Torchwood – Paul Chequer's Body Double

That night I stayed at my friend Greg's house. Gregory is a wonderful actor himself, a beautiful singer, a fantastic guy and was also my voice-over artist for all the Morrison's' in-house films. Greg lived in Bath, which is not too far away from Cardiff.

On the Tuesday morning I came up from Bath and had a whole new location base to go to, at a garden centre near Newport.

It was a bit of a blighter to find, I was still using maps in 2006, not owning a sat-nav, but I managed to get there, told security on the gate who I was and was allowed to park up.

I signed in and was delighted to discover that I had again got my own trailer. Imagine my delight when I found it and discovered that it had my name on the door... well at least it had the words "Eugene Double" on the door. My own trailer for the day, complete with my own call sheet and sides! This was my last day as the Eugene double so I made my mind up to make the most of it.

I changed into costume - a much ripped version of the one that I had worn the day before, (they even gave me some socks!) - Hung my own clothes up in my very own trailer on my very own coat-hanger and placed them on my very own coat hook; (it doesn't take much to please an extra). A few minutes later, there was another knock. Would I like to go to make-up? Make-up was a tad different this time, as the day before Eugene had been cleaned up for his autopsy but today's scenes were from the start of the show where he's lying dead by the river.

 The girls put bruises on my face and hands and a little blood in my hair but that was it to start with and I was sent back into the trailer. There I sat, taking photos of myself for an hour or so (that sounds so wrong, but you get the idea) before I opened the door to see what was going on outside.

As it happens, the police extras all of whom came from a company that specialises in providing such people were just turning up and getting ready. Excellent, there were people to talk to! So I spent the rest of the morning in the bus, until everyone but me went off to the location leaving me alone with more waiting to do. I went back to my trailer.

I had seen John Barrowman briefly so I knew he was there, and I'd seen Paul Chequer and said 'hi' to him. When I look back, how I wish I had had a photo of Paul and me, both in the same outfit.

Another hour or so later the 3rd AD came to take me to location. Instead of the usual minibus it was the actors' car! Nice.

Everyone was there. The camera crew were all set up for the shot. The actors were rehearsing and the police extras were in place. All that was needed was dead Eugene...Me!

James told me where to lie and was good enough to allow me to get into any position that I found comfortable. I did and before I knew it, I had someone tugging my shoe off and someone else pouring blood in my ear, which then ran all down my face and into my mouth. It's actually quite nice. It tastes like sugar!

In the scene John Barrowman has to lift my hand and say what colour car hit me as I had got paint under my finger nails - and yes I really did have paint put onto my nails! John was in a funny mood that day and kept calling me 'dead guy'!

I told him I was demonstrating the difference between going to acting school and not going. There was I, lying in the shit while he was getting his own show! I'll never forget two things in particular about that day. The first thing was JB's farting during takes, while everyone else still stayed in character; the second was a conversation that I had with the star himself. As I lay there with John standing over me, he gave me a wicked look and said: "You could *teabag* me from there."

Now, I'm a naive sort of chap, so I asked him, "John, what is teabag?"

In an instant John jumped to his feet and speaking in his loudest voice for all the cast and crew to hear: "Tea-bagging is when you put your testicles into someone's mouth and they suck while you go up and down."

What could I ever say to that? I just played dead and for just one brief moment, kind of wished I was dead for real.

We chatted a little that day while he was there bending over my dead body. I told him about when I had been offered a speaking role on Hollyoaks In The City as a *cottager*. I had been under the mistaken belief that that was someone who owned a cottage, until someone else had set me straight. "You should have done it," John told me, with his famously sparkly grin.

Then it was back to playing dead again, with more and more blood being poured into my ear and doing the *not really breathing* thing, until it was time for lunch.

There then happened another thing that never happens to extras. I was taken back to base in the car together with some of the actors (albeit I had to sit on a plastic bag so that I didn't drip blood onto the nice seats). When arrived, the 3rd AD offered to fetch my lunch for me in my trailer? This just never happens. Perhaps she was actually a runner on her first day on set, who hadn't yet learnt that she was supposed to treat extras like complete shit! In any case, it was just too much for me, so I queued and got my lunch and sat with the police extras in the bus. I'm not stupid. I know that on my next job I'll be back to sitting in the cold without being told anything, like extras are supposed to be treated!

After lunch I was left behind again until needed but this time it was the mini bus that picked me up. It had started to rain too so I wasn't looking forward to being back in the wet grass! I remember the really cool driver had a photo of me covered in blood.

Back on set, by now the grass had become a mix of make-up and mud! I got back into dead position and held my breath during takes. This was in fact, quite a long scene to hold my breath for and I was starting to have some trouble doing it take after take until the very kind Mr Barrowman pointed out that I was not actually in shot and that they were filming close-ups of the main actors, so I was just there for eye line! I could breathe again.

Then it rained really hard and I was placed in the nice actors' car with Eve Myles and Paul Chequer. Again I had the plastic bag to sit on as the driver wouldn't have been too happy with a bloody corpse in his nice car dripping sugar blood everywhere.

At this point Eve was handed a copy of the newly released latest issue of the Radio Times which featured Torchwood on the cover. I so wanted a signed copy. I'd seen all the cast who were in the cover photo with the exception of Indira Varma. I wondered where she was, not knowing that although the publicity for the launch if Torchwood suggested that she was going to be a regular character, she would, in fact turn out to be the first episode's villain and would not make it into the rest of the series. I sat in the car while Eve phoned her Dad to ask if he had seen the photo, and rather enjoyed being there while she got so excited about making the cover of the Radio Times. She asked if Paul or I had seen it yet.

I also finally got a chance to talk to Paul Chequer and to ask him about "Synchronicity"

Once the rain had stopped, I went back out again onto the by now very wet and so very cold grass. I managed to remember to take my shoe off every time I lay back down and I just tried to get through the rest of the afternoon. Doubling didn't seem quite so exciting any more.

We wrapped and the last I saw of Mr. Barrowman was him shouting, "Goodbye dead guy," as he was driven away.

Back at base I knew that this was my last day, so I was pleased to be asked if I would come back the next day as it was really important. So, I agreed although I had lots of "real" work to catch up on, I was sure one more day wouldn't hurt, plus it looked like they really needed me as not only did the 2nd AD ask but also my agent rang to ask me to go back. It seemed that they really couldn't do without me.

Well I'm not one to let down a Doctor Who spin-off in their hour of need.

Back at Greg's house, it took ages to get the blood out of my hair in the shower. It looked like a scene from Psycho!

Wednesday 18th October 2006 -

Torchwood – Paul Chequer's Body Double

The next day, after all the urgent requests to come back, it turned out that I had never been so unnecessary for a scene in my life. So much for being really needed! It was back to being treated like an extra again too, but then I supposed I'd have to get used to that, as that was the real world.

This time I was in costume in the clean Eugene clothes and even make-up did a clean version of the Eugene 'look'.

"What's the story?" I asked the 3rd AD, as no sides or call-sheets had been given to me.

"Today you and the Gwen double are with the second unit driving her car."

Okay, well make-up were concerned that I might be seen from the front today, so they drew a hairline on me. It's true, they drew a hair line on me just in-case I was seen.

So "Gwen" and I were taken off to some remote roads somewhere, and I just sat in the hire car while she drove. There was a props guy hiding on the floor in the back of the car with the radio giving us instructions and so on. It was just a question of taking some wide shots of Gwen driving home with Eugene tagging along in the car.

The Second Unit were really cool though. They didn't treat us like extras and we all had a nice afternoon just plodding through the shot list.

Dinner was from a big polystyrene box that we all shared. The only worry that day came when the prop guy taking "Gwen" and me back to base stopped to get some petrol and only then realised that he had been driving all the way back with the false TV number plates on.

Back at base I signed out and never came back to first season Torchwood.

10th,11th,13th,14th November 2006 –

Doctor Who: Daleks in Manhattan (Homeless man)

I had been offered Doctor Who again, a job that I would have happily paid them to let me do let alone them paying me, it was a week of night shoots in the mud, the rain and the freezing cold. It was brilliant and I loved it!

The set base for this job was one of the most difficult ones to find yet. I went up and down the same road for hours, but then I didn't make things easy for myself by being so early that there was no security person on the gate to look out for.

I started going down little pathways and side roads in the hope of finding the place, finally striking lucky purely by chance.

Extra Time

It was mid afternoon in Cardiff and I had just posted my latest training film DVD in the mail to the Morrison's Head-office in Bradford. (There is a reason for mentioning that).

I parked up in a field and sat on the Extras bus waiting for more people to turn up and to get into costume, for which I had been fitted the previous week. That was when I discovered that the Daleks were back, as I could hear Nick Briggs (their voice) in the studio next door.

This was a night shoot, so the thermal underwear was needed. On night shoots extras (and everyone else) try to keep warm whenever possible, with never a thought as to whether or not we might look fashionable.

We were to be 1930's poor folk, living in shanty houses in New York's Central Park. Once we were all in costume, and make-up had dirtied us down, we were ready for the set, which was absolutely excellent and was just across the field from us at the back of Cardiff Castle.

I was looking forward finally to meeting Freema, but as a Highlander fan I couldn't believe my luck when Hugh Quarshie turned up on set. To make things even more special, by coincidence this Doctor Who episode was set in the same location as his appearance in Highlander, although for that one, he actually went to the real New York.

David and Freema came onto set and said hello to everyone. I had already discovered that David was so down to earth, and was pleased to find that Freema was just as nice. It must sometimes be difficult for stars like them. Poor David can't even walk down a street these days without being harassed by fans.

I was asked to sit on a chair at the edge of the 'town' which I was amused to notice was called "Hooverville". At the time I wasn't sure if this was a joke name, as film crews tend to call the extras on set "hoovers" because of the way we hoover up any food or biscuits around. Even better, was the fact that that the Doctor Who group that belong to in Derby is called "The Whoovers".

The director on this episode was James Strong, who was very hands on. I was asked if I smoked to which I replied yes. But had I smoked a pipe before? No!

Anyway, the prop guy brought me the pipe, filled it with tobacco and told me that I was going to be the first person on the new Doctor Who to smoke. Is this something to be proud of?

We didn't light it on rehearsal, all I had to do was to watch the Doctor and his companion suspiciously, as they walked through the gates of our town.

While they were setting up, I got to chat to David and Freema quite a lot, as we had the same starting point (called number ones or first positions).

As a long time fan, it was nice to be able to talk about the show to the Doctor, especially about the previous series (David's first).

Freema was brilliant. She knew that she was on a show that would change her life forever and was really proud to be part of it. She told me that she and David had gone to visit a local school, and the kids were all over David, but didn't even want to know her, as she hadn't been on TV yet. It must be weird working on something that everyone will know you for afterwards but not while you are doing it.

I really enjoyed that small moment, until another extra spotted me chatting with them. Everyone knows that extras are not allowed to talk to the actors, and this guy saw his opportunity. I had already done the hard part of breaking the barrier between them and us, so he decided to take advantage.

I had managed to show my enthusiasm without exposing myself as a geek but this guy said some of the worst things imaginable, and proving that he hadn't even seen the new series. He asked if we would go to Gallifrey this season, and even if David would be wearing Tom Baker's scarf! He also managed to insult David, asking if he had got a digital radio set and then when David said that he had, going on about how digital radios use up more power and so are bad for the environment.

No wonder extras get a bad name. As a group we are all only as 'normal' as the most abnormal one among us!

Right, it was time to do the take. I lit my pipe, we turned over and 'action!'

'Cut!'

At the end of the first take, producer Phil Collinson came over to me and said that although they had got permission to smoke the pipe in the show, he had got cold feet. He didn't want me to be cut, so would I hold the pipe without actually lighting it. I was then given a stick from props and spent the next week just cleaning my pipe out.

Lots of these sequences were filmed out of order as we did the day scenes in the afternoon and the night scenes afterwards. We spent the night in the mud, being attacked by Pigmen, who were pretty scary in real life as we didn't see them get into costume before they turned up on set.

They attacked us from all sides, running screaming onto set, (when I say set what I actually mean is mud, mud and more mud) and we had to back into a little group.

After the attack, we turned around, only to be confronted by a flying Dalek!

This was the weirdest thing as the Dalek was in fact just a nicely cut out cardboard Dalek on a big long stick. They were going to CG the Dalek into the finished shot later, although Nick Briggs was on set, doing the Dalek voice through a loud speaker, so it didn't take long to convince me that there was a real Dalek present.

It was one of those moments that I will never forget. Nothing will come close to that experience just standing in the mud under attack from Pig people, with a flying Dalek giving orders from high above the buildings, and the Doctor shouting back offering to sacrifice himself to save the rest of us. I don't think I have ever felt so in the moment before.

The scene cut that night just as the Doctor was screaming at the Dalek (on a stick), "Kill me instead," or something very similar.

How could they end the night at such an exciting point? I wanted to know what was going to happen next but we were wrapped

It was like watching a show with an amazing climax just about to unfold and then turning it off. I couldn't wait to come back the next night to see what happened.

The next evening I sat on a prop chatting with Nick Briggs. I pointed out that it was all his fault that I do extra work. Who would have thought back when we were doing Auton 2, that we would be here together on the set of

Doctor Who? We had really thought it was never coming back. It was kinda nice.

This was the night of the rain. I mean the RAIN! It just wouldn't stop pouring down. In the end we just had to get on and shoot the next scene, despite the rain.

It was the bit where Hugh Quarshie's character "Solomon" tells us that Andrew Garfield's character "Frank" had gone, (which was true, as Andrew Garfield wasn't there that night). So we sat there, take after take, getting soaked through, but typically when they turned the cameras around to get the reverse, it stopped raining!

This posed another problem. For the sake of continuity, we simply had to wait for the rain to start again. In the meantime I used this opportunity, (as a Highlander fan) to talk to Hugh Quarshie about his role in that show. I was worried that I would get the "don't talk to actors" spiel, but not at all, as he was so forthcoming with Highlander information. He talked about the cut scenes and had obviously loved shooting the film.

Finally the rain came back and we got a nice soaking again for the reverse. We jumped back again into yesterday's scene only this time we had lots of explosions and stunts going on, with the second unit shooting at the same time as we were. One unit would cut and the other would call action. It was so well timed between the two units.

The action also continued, so I got to see what happened next, with the Doctor shouting at the Dalek to kill him.

Coming to work every day was such a joy. The next day we started with some green screen work, (if you call walking backwards and forwards work), which was for the wide shots where they put us all on screen together to fill up the city.

Then we did a scene with Eric Loren, whose character was asking us to work for him. I spotted Andrew Garfield and pointed out to Hugh that he wasn't missing after all. He had just had a day off. It seemed funny at the time.

We were all so covered in mud and yet somehow the beautiful Miranda Raison stayed clean, in her white dress throughout the shoot.

While David Tennant and Hugh Quarshie where rehearsing a scene, the first AD came up to me and asked if I would mind playing a joke on them. How could I refuse such an offer?

I went into the prop outside toilet and sat there with my pipe in my mouth and a newspaper as if I was having a number two!

The crew readjusted some lighting to make me show up. It wasn't until the next rehearsal that DT spotted me and burst into laughter. The first AD told me someone had recorded it but if they ever did, I have never seen the footage.

Before coming to work on the third night I got a call from work (my real job at Morrisons) and although I was having a week holiday, they told me that the DVD I had sent them in the mail hadn't turned up. They needed another copy of the training film by first thing in the morning.

Extra Time

When we wrapped in the early hours, I had to drive from Cardiff to Derbyshire to make another disc of this training film and then on to Bradford to drop it off. I only just made it back to Cardiff to get straight back to work. I was a tad tired

Just when I thought things couldn't get any better, I was picked for a featured role, was this because of my love of the show? My talent? My looks? None of the above I'm afraid, it was just how it happened to work.

I was on the extras bus minding my own business except for finding out what other episodes the other extras had done, when someone came rushing in asking us all to show her our arms. She was looking for a white arm without much hair on it!

One look at mine and she grabbed me and hauled me into the production office so that the director James Strong and producer Phil Collinson could check that my arm was up to the job!

The best part of it was that I got to sit in the dry with Freema and Miranda while the others had to walk around in the rain.

I'd been to make-up (the actors make-up trailer and not the usual extras one), and they had put a really nice burn mark onto my arm.

In the scene, Freema is supposed to put a bandage on my burn, although the real on-set medic pointed out that in real life you would never do that. So, it was decided that my injury wasn't a burn after all, and Freema was allowed to bandage it up. I guess we have to assume it was some sort of nasty Dalek war wound!

Earl Perkins (another actor on set) was helping me master my American accent. It'll never happen. I'll never pass as an American!

So, Freema did her stuff, telling me to look after the arm or something and I got to say my only dialogue on the show ever. In my best American accent I said, "thanks" put my hat on and walked off

Would you believe it, when I saw the show on broadcast, my line had been dubbed over!

I drove home the following morning having been up over 50 hours but in such a state of excitement that I didn't realize how tired I was until I was in bed.

11th January 2007 – Hollyoaks (Paramedic)

I've not included many soap stories here as they all seem to blend into one but this particular day on Hollyoaks will never be forgotten.

I got a call to play a Paramedic on the show and so I drove to the studios on the outskirts of Liverpool to do this nice small role.

Back in 2007, Grange Hill was still on TV, being shot in the same studios. I never did get to go on that show or even to take a photo of the school with the big large "GRANGE HILL" lettering at the side but I did get to smoke by the bike sheds, just to be able to say that I'd done it!

Sorry, I digressed. Anyway, I had become a paramedic, one of two that day.

The story was that some woman had had a baby on the kitchen floor; however we were luckily on hand to deliver it!

We were called to set and my fellow extra was asked to do some medic stuff with the actress while I was given the ugliest heavy little rubber baby ever. My role was to pass the baby back to the mother's sister, as it seemed we had arrived there in time to do a check up, but just a little too late to deliver it.

I was to walk back in and give the baby back to the sister who was sitting in a chair facing camera. This was good, as I would be back to camera and it would be easy to hide the rubber baby!

We rehearsed for this several times before the 1st AD happened to remark to me, "John, you are aware this is going to be a real baby, aren't you?"

I laughed at his funny joke. Well, extras are expected to laugh at all crew or actors' attempts at humour at all times.

He looked at me and said, "No, really, we've got a real baby coming in now"

I panicked. I'd never held an actual baby before. I had never held a real baby in real life and here I was about to do it in front of cameras for a TV soap!

I was terrified. What if I broke it, or dropped it, or something.

The baby's mother found it all very amusing and passed him/her (I can't remember which, but I guess it was one or the other) to me and... He/she didn't cry!

When we did the scene for real, it took a few seconds longer than it should have as I didn't want to break or damage the baby, but no one complained.

Sunday 18th March 2007 – The Whistleblowers (Laywer)

I only wanted to mention this job because it was another when they held me back all day, as I was going to be heavily featured! It was in London at the Kingston- upon-Thames Court House, as usual.

The show starred Richard Coyle and the beautiful Torchwood actress Indira Varma. It turned out to be a brilliant show.

I'd not had the chance to see Indira on the Torchwood set so I was very happy to get this small "walk-on".

There were three actors plus me in the scene, two of us on each side of the court with the public sitting behind us. Unfortunately the actor playing the defence lawyer and myself were on the opposite side to Indira, but nonetheless I was quite excited by the role.

The defence lawyer and I had to be given a message about something, which we had to look at and then do some pretend talking.

Sometimes we extras forget our place and believe we're of some sort of value to a TV show or film above being a breathing prop, or moving scenery as we're also known. However, there is a reason why productions use extras instead of real actors as walk-ons. It's because the role isn't particularly important, and it would be wrong to get an actor in for something that could quite easily be cut.

When the show was broadcast, I enjoyed every episode, which is quite unusual for me when it comes to TV that's not Science Fiction or cult in nature.

When it came to my episode near the end of the series, they had somehow cut me right out, to the point that the cameraman had never even framed me in shot. After so much attention to detail, with my suit and make-up and facial expressions, I wasn't even in the show.

I turned it off and never watched it again, although I don't think I was to blame for it not being commissioned for a second series. I had had another reminder that you can never assume that you're going to be in a show, no matter how big your role is, until you actually see it on screen.

Tuesday 27th March 2007- HSC Advert (Vegetable Man)

This job came out of the blue and I don't really know why I got it. When I got the call from the agent, I thought she'd said an HSBC advert so I guessed I'd be playing some sort of bank guy, but they called back nearer the time and gave me some more information.

"Please wear a smart suit..." I'd guessed that much, but the next bit took me by surprise a little, "...and don't bother getting your hair cut as your head will be a vegetable!"

I double checked that I had heard that bit of information correctly, and yes, I was getting a vegetable head!

The location was based in an MOD site with "DO NOT ENTER" in large letters on the front gate. It was misty and I was looking for Hanger J - very X-Files!

I had a little trouble finding it, so I decided to stop and ask someone. There weren't many people around at this time in the morning. I had expected masses of security with guns but alas no. Then I saw someone. I stopped the car, opened the window and asked if he knew where I could find Hanger J.

To make this even more Mulder and Scully, he had no idea!

Then I saw someone else who looked lost, driving around in the mist, whom I guessed was one of us!

We stopped and decided to start a mini convoy. How hard could it be? Hanger H, Hanger I, Hanger K...Hanger K? Where was J?

We finally found it down a side road off the main hanger track.

The set consisted simply of a bus, a catering truck and the mobile production office, plus the main hanger - Hanger J

The hanger was a large, well-lit building that was being used for parking cars. I had expected a large UFO prop or something.

The actual set turned out to be a tiny hanging green screen and a shopping trolley.

We were introduced to the director. You always know it's a small and friendly set when the director talks to you.

There were only six extras in that day, and no actors. All we were doing was pretending to be vegetables in suits, running around or fighting, but disappointingly, we didn't get vegetable heads, they were being added on by CGI, in post-production. They had us go onto the set, in front of the green screen, and do our thing, one at a time.

It turned out to be a really good day. I met some really nice fellow extras who have become friends (when I say friends I actually mean working colleges that I'll never speak to again when I give this job up), and talked Doctor Who.

The production company could have easily just used one of us, putting a different vegetable head on each time, but they paid us very well for what was a very fast and simple job.

I was in no hurry to finish, so I waited until last to go on and did my bit, which involved holding onto a pole and waggling my feet. I did this twice for about ten seconds a time, and that was it, I was wrapped. They were going to CG us from the waist up and I was going to be a flying vegetable!

I don't think the production company expected to be finished so early, but they asked if we wanted to stay for lunch or go home. The food was so amazing that it would have been rude to leave it.

Tuesday 5th June 2007 –

Shoot on sight (Policeman or Policewoman's Husband)

I didn't realise this was a movie until I got to the set. It was filmed in a town centre and there were masses of extras. We had to bring a dinner suit and I popped out to get a bow tie as well, as all I had was the type that fixes together at the back.

While we were getting ready, we were told that this was going to be a rather controversial film, based on the story of Jean Charles de Menezes, the Brazilian electrician who was shot and killed by officers of the Metropolitan Police in Stockwell Underground Station in 2005, in the belief that he was a terrorist. Today we were all going to be police officers or their partners at a Policeman's Ball.

For the life of me, I cannot remember why I had a moustache and no beard at that time. I looked like a porn actor from the 1970s. For some reason I kept this porn moustache for a few weeks. If anyone knows why I did this, please let me know!

The great thing about TV is you never know who your TV/Film partner/wife/boyfriend is going to be and on this occasion, for some very strange reason, I was put with a real ex-page three girl, complete with low cut top. So together, we now looked more like a pair of porn stars than we did police.

I can't remember the young lady's name but she was there with her boyfriend, who was a fireman. Typically, the ADs put her with someone she didn't know. Namely me!

Extra Time

We were in a group of about 40 extras, and got on really well - though not well enough for me to remember her name, it seems.

The scene involved the main actors walking up the stairs towards dinner with all the guests in a line behind. It was nothing special at all.

Costume just couldn't leave my bow-tie alone as it kept creeping sideways. In the end they swapped it for one of those fake ones that clip together at the back! So much for making an effort!

We started the scene and the main actors made their way up the stairs. Everybody had been given a number so we knew whom we were to follow.

The young lady and myself were right at the end, so as we were not even going to make it to the stairs, we didn't bother listening to the instructions about how far away from the person in front we should stand, and so on.

They did a couple of takes and we just meandered around at the base of the stairs, as the scene was cut before we even moved.

Suddenly, half way through a take the director called cut and went mad at some extra for wearing a rubbish dinner suit!

The poor man was humiliated and told to go into the other room and wait with the other unused extras.

Without warning my new porn wife and I were told to go and take his place directly behind the main actors!

"Straight away from the top, turn over and action!" calls the 1st AD

We had no idea whatsoever about what we were supposed to do, and as the scene didn't have any dialogue in it we were allowed to speak.

We found that we got on really well, as if we'd known each other for years so within minutes we were having friendly debates.

Standing in front of us was Greta Scacchi. We didn't realise that she'd been listening to everything we had said, until she started to talk to us. She assumed we were a real couple so we must have been doing a good job of pretending. She also seemed to be amused that we looked like porn stars rather than police.

At lunch time my "partner's" boyfriend had to go to the fire station and so she had to leave too as he was her lift home. I was suddenly without wife!

Lunch was outside and was the first time that I'd ever seen an extra stealing food and drinks and putting them into his bag! Extras were getting photos taken with Greta and Brian Cox (if I even attempted to do that, I'd be the one caught and sacked!)

After stuffing our faces at dinner, the very next scene that had all the extras in it was in fact an eating scene.

We were put into a massive room with food laid out for everyone.

Usually, we're told not to eat the food. On Coronation Street we are usually told that the cakes are out of date, so we shouldn't eat them for our own sake, although I remember I was allowed to eat a cheese sandwich that Vera Duckworth had made for me. It was just two pieces of bread with a serious amount of grated cheese in the middle. I decided not to actually eat that one. Oh, and if you ever have a hot drink, don't sip it as it'll be so cold by take eight.

We were given seats, but there was a gap where my wife should have been, so a new wife was brought from the back of the room and placed there.

The camera seemed to be on our side of the table quite a lot and we were asked to eat. Now, there's only so much you can eat for TV time and time again. I still have yet to see this film and I'm not really one for telling people what jobs I've done (until now). I hadn't told anyone about that scene, but a while later I got a call from a friend in London who said he'd seen me on at the cinema and he mentioned both of those scenes, so they must have made it into the film.

That reminds me of a time when I was on Waterloo Road. Eva Pope and I were eating at a buffet. We had a small quarter sandwich each and Philip Martin Brown, who plays Grantly came up to us both and said that he hadn't touched anything, as you never know how many takes they would have to do. I thought that if a professional like Eva Pope knew what she was doing then why wouldn't I just copy her. Sure enough, they filmed every angle and several takes, by the end of which we were both stuffed and feeling quite sick. We then started to fake it and hid our faces a little, as we simply couldn't eat any more.

Friday 3rd August 2007 –

Benefit Fraud Poster Campaign (Fraudster)

My northern agent had called to say that I had been picked to be in a poster campaign for Benefit Fraud (against it, rather than promoting it). He actually knew me and what I was capable of and so had always given me work that suited me rather than just random jobs, like the other agents did. I still have agents to this day that have no idea who I am as well as other agents who know who I am but don't give a monkey's. At the end of the day all extras are eminently replaceable and you're either used or you're not. Being an extra, (as I've said before), is the only job I can think of where there is no progression and no promotion. It doesn't matter if you have been doing it for a week or for forty years; you end up where you started.

So everything was going well with my Manchester agent, and I was getting nice jobs, until one day without warning he upped and left. Suddenly, all that personal touch just vanished. It was back to just getting random jobs. But that was all in the future, I've just jumped a year or so ahead. Sorry.

The Benefit Fraud guys actually did some homework on me to find out if I had ever claimed benefit – which I hadn't; so I was cool to be the naughty chap in the poster who is cheating the system by working and claiming at the same time!

I was met outside the agency by a young man whom I asked where the poster would be going. His answer was to point at the lamppost next to us, "Everywhere". He had been on the previous poster, himself. That was weird to be standing, talking to someone who is on a poster on the lampposts and telephone boxes next to you!

He took me into his car and we met the crew of about five people on location up some back street outside of town.

It took a while until costume were happy with my outfit, but the boots I wore belonged to the photographer and were way too big for me. I couldn't actually walk but as it was a still shoot, it didn't matter.

It took about two hours to do the shoot, which was spent mostly walking up and down the road, in different outfits, being photographed from different angles.

In the following months I kind of forgot about this job, until about six months later, I was driving home from Manchester and there in front of me, on a bus shelter was my photo! I stopped the car, got out and took photos of it. After that I began seeing it all around the country, my favourite location being in Waterloo between the National Theatre and the Old Vic.

I still stopped to take photos of all the posters I saw, with rather boring results as all bus shelters kind of look the same. Although I tried to get a real poster of my own, I never managed to.

People must have thought that I was somewhat weird, taking photos of bus posters. I even got a stranger to take one of me with the poster once, but I did tell him why, and am pleased to report that he didn't run off with the camera!

Wednesday 8th August 2007 – Waterloo Road (Teacher)

This was the first time I ever did Waterloo Road. It was filmed in Rochadale and set in a secondary school. In fact I did Waterloo Road for a few years, playing one of the teachers. I love shows like this as the extras are just as invisible on screen as they are in real life. I'll give some examples and if you've not noticed this before, you will now.

My first time on the show wasn't actually in the school; it was at a pub in Rochdale. I was the only extra booked that day to play a teacher as all the others were playing pub regulars.

This meant that I had to be with the actors playing the teachers in the pub. It seemed we were having a night out without inviting our head teacher. It's a show that I've never had a chance to watch, so I didn't know who was who.

It was karaoke night and the teachers (actors) all had a pre-recorded song to sing along to. We all sat and watched while several cast members had conversations. Even though I was sitting with them, as I was just an extra, there was nothing in the script to suggest that anyone was to acknowledge me or even to notice that I was there. So I had to sit and pretend to be having a wonderful time with a bunch of teachers who didn't even acknowledge my existence.

The day was really nice though, and the crew were amazing. There were a couple of actors I really got to like, although there were one or two who never gave me eye contact in the two years I did on this show.

To keep the eye line in the right place, rather than get the actors to take their place on the karaoke stage and mime out of shot, Andi the first AD, (who became known as Andi the Girl after she left and was replaced by a male 3rd AD called Andy) stood in and did the mime for us to look at, earning our respect forevermore.

Our favourite days on Waterloo Road were spent in the staff room. Have a look at the list of who has what coffee or tea on the notice board. It's only the characters who are played by proper actors, whose names are up there. Also when there's a conversation in the staffroom, it's only those characters that join in. We just nod! We are never acknowledged, or asked to make the coffee, or offered a coffee in return. We are never spoken to in the corridors and all the 'proper characters' sit together in the centre of the room. If there is a gap in the chairs, an extra is thrown in but always appears too involved in an out-of-date magazine to make a comment or listen in. We also always happen to walk away, just in time to allow private conversations to take place!

One of the jobs I used to love on that show was taking a set of exercise books and putting names on them, filling out tests, and making every book look different so that we could mark them in other scenes. I know that seems really sad, and I'm sure real teachers have better things to do with their time, but they would get us in at seven in the morning, no matter what time we would eventually be needed, so we would have to sit there with nothing to do, never wrapping before six o'clock at night.

One of the things I didn't like about Waterloo Road was that sometimes they could surprise us by deciding that a scene from an older episode needed to be picked up, so we would have to bring lots of clothes in with us.

Now and again if I was working two days in a row, I would sleep in the car and get cleaned in the school toilets in the morning.

A crew member once told me that I ought to stay in the school at the house set, but I wasn't so sure that the producer would find that very acceptable, so the car was good enough for me.

Once, early in series six (or thereabouts), I had to put a post-it note on the staff notice board for a scene. In 'TV World', it's very important that the correct people do the correct jobs, so the prop department were asked to make the note for me to use.

I was quite pleased that day because I found out that my character had a name (extras get very excited if we are given names). My post-it note said something like "If you see a black briefcase, please return it to Neil."

It stayed up on that board until the end of the season, and could still be there now for all I know, but it's only now as I'm writing this that I realize that the props guy was called Neil. He wasn't giving me a name; he had just put his own name on the note!

Tuesday 21st August/ Wed 22nd August 2007 –

Doctor Who: Planet of the Ood. (Sales Rep)

I love it so much when I get Doctor Who. To this day I still can't believe they actually pay me to go on the show. I'm sure that if they charged people to be on it, they'd never have to pay another extra again and they'd make a fortune!

By now I'd come to know some of the crew members, and they knew that I was a big fan. Arriving early as usual, I was told to wait on the extras bus, but this was Doctor Who Central, the main base at Trefforest Industrial Estate. Why in the world would I want to sit on a bus when I could stand outside and see what bits of information I could pick up.

The very first thing I saw that morning was the Ood heads being moved from set to set. I knew the prosthetics guy so I thought I'd go and say hello, just to get a good close up look at a head! (For those who don't know, an Ood is one of the most successful races of aliens that have been created for the new series of Doctor Who, with a bald head, flashing red eyes and a mess of tentacles where its mouth should be).

It turned out that they were for going to be used that very day and that we too would be in the new Ood episode, filming in studio all day.

This was what I had been hoping for, as the director of this episode was the very well respected Graeme Harper, a near-legend among Doctor Who fans. I had filmed Graeme, giving a talk at the Whoovers Doctor Who Group in Derby a few weeks earlier, and had promised him a preview copy of the disc prior to its release. (The DVD is still available from the Whoovers, all profits go back to the group. Look them up on the internet)

When Graeme turned up, I said good morning and promptly gave him his disc. He looked scared to death "John, What on earth are you doing here?" he asked dumbfounded.

"Didn't I mention that I'm an extra?" I replied.

Of course I hadn't mentioned that I was an extra. If you want to lose any respect you have as a human being, then simply tell any actor or crew member, or even better any director that you're an extra!

Other people outside the industry, (I say that as if I'm in the industry), still don't get this and when we get guests at the Doctor Who Group people always like to tell them what I do, as if they will be impressed!

Before 2005 being a Doctor Who fan was almost something to be ashamed of. We were often ridiculed for it. Then, almost overnight, when the new series started, it became cool. (Although perhaps being a forty year old fan isn't quite that cool). I had always held my head up high and said, "Yes I love Doctor Who and other science-fiction related programmes."

I gave Graeme the disc and went back to my spotting position near the smoking area to see what else I could see.

The other extras turned up and we got on quite well although as usual, I was the only fan of the show. The others were intrigued as to why I love it so much.

We all came from the same agency except one! (Tony, you know I think you're brilliant but I so wanted that role!)

Tony came in from another extras agency and was booked to have a couple of lines! I wanted those lines! You can now see that I'm like a spoilt child but I've promised I won't lie in this book.

We went to costume. We had been given instructions to bring a suit but they had suits, shirts and ties all ready for each of us. The collars, which were like the ones we wear on period shows, hurt like mad.

They don't like us taking photos on Doctor Who (or most other shows for that matter) but I managed to persuade my friend Rhys to come around the corner so we could take sneaky photos of each other. Rhys is on the one on the trading card, by the way.

This was the first time that I had seen Catherine Tate working. I had been told that she was quite a quiet person, but I suppose I was still expecting her to be like she is on her comedy show on TV. She was indeed a very private person and it was David Tennant who was a little more outgoing than usual.

Extra Time

We were finally brought into the studio and onto set. It wasn't very big but the detail was amazing. We were given Ood sales and information books by the prop department, which were fantastic. The prop department made sure that every one of them was counted back in every time we left set, just to make sure that we didn't steal them.

The first few scenes were simply us all walking around the set inspecting the Ood. It was brilliant to see Graeme working, shouting before every take "Lots of energy, lots of pace."

I'm not really into many TV comedy sketch shows but I love the Catherine Tate Show and wish I had been an extra in that show when it was on. Now here I was, in one particular scene; standing right behind Catherine while she was talking to Paul Kasey dressed as an Ood, giving it her full TV persona. It was lucky that we do rehearsals as I burst out laughing.

I've always prided myself on being able to keep a straight face in any situation but on this occasion, I was really struggling.

I knew they'd remove me from the scene if I laughed, so I managed to hold it together in the take. Sure enough, straight away after the take Catherine went back into quiet mode.

David on the other hand stood up on an Ood plinth and decided to dance for one of the camera men, singing "I'm your private dancer" whilst looking down the lens. It's a shame they weren't recording it!

Meanwhile, while one extra and I were still on set, all the other extras were off having an official photo shoot!

I got chatting that day to an actor called Tariq Jordan who not only played the Sales Rep leader, but also turned out to be the brother of Yasmin

Paige, who starred as Maria in the first series of Doctor Who spin-off The Sarah Jane Adventures.

The next day was pretty much the same thing, walking around looking at the Ood and listening to Ayesha Dharker, who played Solana. Tony got to do his line (Bah! Humbug!) and to make things even worse, he was actually pretty good for an extra.

The afternoon became far more exciting, as we were all being killed off. That was so much fun. Each time that someone was getting their close up, dying, the rest of us were running backwards and forwards behind them screaming. Only to be honest, we were more laughing and seeing whom you could knock over by smashing into them, than actually panicking.

I spoke to one of the guys who played an Ood and asked if he had done the Cyberman casting back when I had done it. He had, but he said that many of the guys who had played Cybermen had since dropped out, so the agency were now just getting anybody, regardless of whether they'd been to the casting or not.

We were booked to come back on the show for external scenes, but at the time I knew nothing more than that.

When I got home I dropped the most unsubtle of e-mails to the agency, pointing out I had done skin work, I was slim and of the right height, so please could they consider me for any monster roles. Alas, I am still waiting for a reply!

Tuesday 28th August 2007 - Lewis (Reporter)

Lewis is one of those shows that I do quite often, but I never take any notice of which episodes I have done as I have never watched the show.

On this particular day I had a line to say. It was just typical that they would give me lines in a show that I never watch. "Inspector Lewis, can you tell me how many officers you have on the scene?", but I never get lines on Doctor Who. (I really am like a spoilt child).

On another occasion on Lewis, it was a really wet, in fact it was pouring down. We were filming inside a museum, or at least in somewhere that was set up to look like a museum.

As I sat there, I saw a very wet young lady walk in at the back of the hall with a hood over her face and a KFC in her hand. I said to the guy next to me, "Look, there's Billy Piper." He wouldn't believe me. "Why would Billy Piper be here? She's not in this show and she wouldn't look like that."

I pointed out whom she was dating, (they're now married). She could afford to look very wet because she was not in the show. As she kissed Laurence Fox and turned to go, the guy next to me finally believed me!

We then got up to do the scene. At the time I had a full time job, as I have mentioned before with a company mobile phone. I didn't want to change my number so I always carried both telephones on me. On set we are told to have our telephones turned off at all times, which seemed silly to me for two reasons.

1. How do I know if someone is calling me if my mobile is off?

2. How come the crew are allowed to keep theirs on? How can you tell me that extras' telephones affect the boom mike, when other people's don't?

So, I had mine on silent.

We were all facing forwards while one of the actors gave us a speech, when they called cut early as there was phone interference.

The AD shouted at all the extras, saying that we shouldn't have our phones turned on while on set nor in fact have them with us at all!

He made such a point of it that we all took our phones out of our pockets and made sure they were switched off. "Not on Silent – Off!"

Of course I just checked that both of mine were on silent!

The scene started again and once again it was cut early as the sound guy said that there was definitely a mobile phone switched on in the building. This time the crew had to turn theirs off too. I took the hint and turned my private phone off, leaving my work one turned on just in case someone wanted to get hold of me!

The scene started again and once again they cut it due to interference.

This time the AD was so mad, he came right up to the extras, stood right in front of us and said we'd not turned our phones off and we were wasting their time. Lunch would be delayed because of it. I felt my pocket vibrating! Someone was trying to get hold of me. I couldn't believe no one else could hear the vibrating but it was too late to turn it off now. Imagine getting the phone out after such a shouting at and turning it off! I'd have been thrown off set. It was best to say nothing and hope they wouldn't notice.

Before you know it, we were being told to take our phones out of our pockets and hold them up. We had to show that our phones were switched off. I took my private phone out and left the other one where it was, wondering who had phoned and wanting to check it.

The 3rd AD reported to the 1st AD that it was none of the extras and they finally decided that the interference must have been coming from outside the building and that the extras were innocent after all. They apologised.

Tuesday 4th September 2007 –

Doctor Who Planet of the Ood (Sales Rep)

This was a location shoot based inside a closed down factory site, which again took a while to find, although I did find the old Doctor Who studios around the corner. It looked like no one had been back there since Doctor Who moved out. I wondered what treasures had been left behind for the next residents.

As ever, I was very early, but several of the crew members knew me and were happy to let me sit down on the side and watch the filming, which was nice of them. There were solders running around shooting Ood and the like, all in a big fake snow drift which had been brought in for the location. It looked so real despite it being one of those abnormally hot September days.

I saw Graeme and he said hello. I said that I knew it wasn't protocol, but would he mind autographing his new book for me later on. He said he'd be delighted to and told me to catch him after the shoot.

The other extras from my group started arriving and we were sent to the costume truck to get ready.

The difference this time was that we got to use our own coats. I asked if I was allowed to wear my own gloves too, as they were among the few items of clothing that I owned that had yet to be on TV! Come to think of it, I've got a coat too that hasn't been on TV (yet), but that's a special case. It was actually made for and used in the film Highlander 4, (did I mention how much of a Highlander fan I am?), and one day I will wear it on TV but you would have to see it to understand why it's been a tad difficult so far.

I wasn't really used in this episode. That's the thing with this job, some days you're used a lot, while others you are simply forgotten, (sometimes deliberately).

In the main scene that I was in, we had to form a queue to meet our hosts. I was standing near the back talking politely to Tariq.

The 3rd AD came along and told us both to get to the front of the queue.

A couple of extras who had found it funny that I wasn't being used much on this episode gave me the thumbs up, as they were genuinely pleased for me, knowing as they did how much I loved the show.

So, I was told that I would be handing out the booklets and information packs to the other Sales Reps. Then the 3rd spotted Tony the talking extra in the queue. She had confused me with him and shouted over to me. "John, get back where you were, Tony should be doing that!" So I returned to the back with the other guys and it became a joke again. Not to worry. If I never did another episode of Doctor Who, at least I can say that I've had some fun on the show up to now.

We had to stand there in the scene looking really cold, which is surprisingly difficult in such hot weather wearing the tightest collars ever plus our coats and gloves.

We weren't on set for long, so figuring that I wouldn't be back on the show for a while, I took the opportunity to go and see Graeme Harper. I went to the production office taking with me my copy of his new book about directing Doctor Who, 'Calling The Shots'.

When I knocked on the door, a production assistant answered and gave me a look of pure disdain. Before she said a word, the message was clear, "What the hell was an extra doing knocking on the production office door?" Anyway, I took a breath and asked if Graeme was busy. Before she could tell me that he was a shout came from within, "Come on in".

She moved out of the way and I went up the stairs into the office. I thanked Graeme for having me on his episode and he signed my book. I know the director doesn't make the decisions about what extras are or are not in the show, and I'm under no illusions that he'll ever remember me again, but it never hurts to be polite.

The old studio, now empty. I wonder what Doctor Who props are still in that skip?

Thursday 20th September 2007 –

Emmerdale (Doctor/ Detective)

This was a weird day. There is a rule on TV soaps, which says that unless you are playing a regular or recurring character, once you have appeared on a show, you are not allowed back onto the same show for six to eight weeks (it varies from show to show). This applies even if you only appeared in the deep background, with your back to camera. It happened to me recently that I had been booked for Casualty, but as it happened I wasn't used. Nonetheless, my agency still wouldn't let me back on until I had served my time out.

Having said all that, there I was on Emmerdale, having played a doctor on the show for about four years, now playing a detective. I know you're probably thinking that no one but my booker at the agency would even know that I'd been playing a Doctor on the show for a while, so why would it matter that I had now turned into a detective? Well, the odd thing was that I was playing the two different parts, in two consecutive episodes, shown on two consecutive days – and I got a nice big close up for both characters! The rules seem to change when you're on set.

Anyway, the role of the doctor was nothing different from the usual, standing there, chatting in the corridor failing to notice a girl, sneaking into the hospital to visit someone. By the way, I was paired in this scene with my new TV partner Helen, replacing Monica, who had disappeared for some reason that I never found out.

Then in the afternoon, we went to the police station set at the back of YTV to film a scene in which one of the guest actresses is talking to some police officers, when she starts to cry, and then bursts out of the office door and runs past the camera.

I started the scene sitting at my police desk doing some paper work and then on cue, I got up and walked away so that the camera got a clear view of her. The camera was only supposed to be on me for the establishing shot and for the part when she runs out of the room, after which I should have gone.

When I am given a desk to sit at, I have a tendency to become quite anal and to make it my very own! I think this is just another case of an extra needing something a little more substantial than background work. So, the first thing I do is tidy the desk up and put my own mobile phone onto it! This is something that I have always done, and I make no apology for it. More often than not, the props guys then do their job and mess it up again, but they have been known to make a super tidy desk just for me. Recently I did a show called Scott and Bailey and they left the same Dime Bar wrapper on my desk for the entire 6 episode run, which was supposed to be over 7 months!

So, on the first take, I got into my chair, got my telephone out, tidied up a bit, worked on the computer, answered the phone and left my seat on the appropriate line.

The director wasn't pleased with my performance. Apparently I was way too 'busy' and was moving too fast. I just had to slow it down. I guess I'm just not used to having the entire crew sitting in face forwards in front of me, with the actors in my background.

So, I slowed it down just like I was asked. The poor actress had spent the entire scene working her way up into full out crying mode and I had messed it up for her.

Take two. I got into my chair, slowly took my telephone out of my pocket, turned in a leisurely manner to the computer and answered the phone while all the time trying to hear the dialogue so I could go on my cue.

I must have missed it. They were saying things that came after the point at which I should have gone. Then I heard the crew speaking. "He should have gone" "He didn't get up" "The guy's still in his chair."

I didn't know what to do. I was panicking. Extras are not supposed to panic. We are paid reasonably well for doing pretty much nothing and now I had messed it up. I didn't know what to do!

"Shall I get up now, even though it's not the right time?" I was thinking "Or should I just sit here, because I'm not supposed to move unless she says that line... which she's already said!"

I was panicking so much that I just froze. The actress got all worked up again and burst into tears and came running out of the office, past me and off past the camera.

The 1st AD came up to me. I could already see the disappointed faces of the crew and I knew I was about to be made to look smaller than I already felt!

"Could you not hear the dialogue? Do you know your cue?" He asked.

"Sorry sir, I didn't hear the line."

"OK, well next time don't worry if you miss it. Just make sure you're out of that seat and out of shot before she leaves the room!"

"OK."

I felt really stupid. I was just helping to prove that all extras are thick! I apologised to the actress as she walked past me and back into the office but she blanked me. Either she hated me too or she was in character so couldn't speak to me.

I got it right the next take. I guess if I hadn't I wouldn't be here now

Friday 28th September 2007 - Young Victoria (Builder)

I got a call from my London agency asking if I would like to go to Lincoln to do a day on Young Victoria starring Emily Blunt, although if I did, I would have to pop up there for a costume fitting first.

If I had relied on this job as a living back in 2007 then I would never had gone to Lincoln twice, two days just for a fitting and one day filming, but I had been quite busy with my real job of late and hadn't done as much extra work as I would have liked, so I jumped at the chance.

I was fitted as a builder and I got to wear a wig, which was cool as my own hair has receded over the years, so a toupé provides me with an instant hairline. The sad part of being wigged however is that although one can deal with receding hair, after all it happens over a number of years so doesn't come as a shock you when you look in the mirror each day; a wig makes for instant receding the moment it is taken off.

Anyway, I had my wig and some nice cool chops on the side of my face so I was very pleased with the make-up.

There were about eight of us playing builder types but when I spoke to the others, it turned out that they weren't real extras, they were local people pretending to be extras, who had answered an advert in the local paper. I seemed to be the only real extra among them. Can you see that extras' superiority thing happening to me there.

We weren't needed for most of the day, but it was fun talking to the new guys. When we were finally called to set, a request had been sent to the costume department to find the best dressed 'down' extra, to be given a line! I'd never spoken on an actual movie before as I'd mainly done TV and mostly soaps at that, so I was keen for this opportunity to speak, or even be featured on a movie. I always tell other extras who want to be featured that they should learn to act and then they might have a chance, but on that day, I knew that it could be any one of us whom was chosen.

Costume ended up picking me and someone else for the director to choose from. A fifty-fifty chance but I was still not holding my breath as I'd learned by now that if you want something bad enough, you'll never get it!

I love it when I'm in a room and the 3rd AD pops in to say that they'll be picking someone for a featured role. Truth be told, they've usually decided whom they want already, but the extras, especially the new ones and the ass kissing keen ones, get all excited and will happily stab each other in the back, doing their best to catch the eye of the AD. I'm afraid I'm like that in Doctor Who. I may not be proud of my over-keen behaviour, but at least I'm honest about it.

So, the two of us were kept behind as the other extras were placed in the scene, which was being filmed in a church. Scaffolding had been erected with a wooden skin to make it look period, as the church was doubling for Westminster Abbey in the mid nineteenth century.

Extra Time

The other guy and I were brought in and the 1st AD asked the question "Are either of you scared of heights?"

Me being Mr Keen and knowing full well that the other chap wasn't a real extra and wasn't experienced in speaking as quick as you can to get in there first said "I'm not"

Of course I'd said this thinking that being given the featured role meant being somewhere high. Heights aren't my favourite thing but hey, this is the movies!

The 1st seemed very pleased with me and promptly asked me to climb the ladder so I could be a silhouette against the window, while the other guy was given the speaking role! (Note, don't be too eager!)

The other chap got to speak to Emily Blunt as she came in "Good morning, Your Highness," or something like that.

After a rehearsal there was a change of plan. Now we all had to say, "Your Highness" as she walked in. It may not be a featured role, but that is still classed as speaking on a movie!

Well, we tried it and then it was changed back to just the one chap speaking.

The thing is when you are featured, you can't be used again or the audience will recognise you, but all those extras whose faces were not seen had to stay all day just to be walking around in the other angled shots, while speaky boy got paid more, got featured and got to go home early!

Wednesday 21st November 2007 –

Torchwood (Captain John Double)

Series 2 of Torchwood had pretty much finished filming, without me even getting a sniff at being on it. In fact I thought the series had already wrapped when I got a call asking if I would double for an actor called James Marsters. I was concerned that I didn't have the white bleached hair that he had worn when playing Spike in *Buffy The Vampire* Slayer and *Angel,* but it turned out that had gone.

Let me explain the difference between a 'looky-likey', a 'stand in' and a 'double'.

A looky-likey is someone who actually looks physically like someone else and is used when the likes of Prince William or David Beckham are too expensive to get. A looky-likey is brought in to show their face on screen and pretend to be that character.

A stand-in doesn't have to look like the actor who they are standing in for at all, in fact they don't even have to be the same sex as the actor they're standing in for. The correct skin colour and height do help, as a stand in is used to get the camera angle, lights, scene set up and so on, without the real actor having to stand there doing nothing. Sometimes, especially on films, it can take a long time to set up a shot, so the actors can relax in their trailers, leaving the set up for the stand-in.

A double, which is what I was booked as, tends to be the same build as the actor so that they can fit into the actor's clothes, and may have certain physical features similar to them, so allowing the crew to film around the double without viewers noticing that it's not the same person. When someone doubles an actor, the actor isn't usually around or is busy on another block filming a sequence where their face is seen.

Doubles simply save money for the production. Did you really think that an expensive actor was driving that car that you could see in the distance? Or did you think that the hand that was picking something up was that of an actor, when a "pick-up shot" is usually filmed by a different crew on a different day and in many cases in a different place.

I was doubling that day because James Marsters was in America and the shots were a reverse of his conversation with John Barrowman, which had already been filmed.

I got to the Doctor Who Cardiff studios early as always and soon found out that I was the only extra on Torchwood that day although Doctor Who was filming there too.

Doctor Who was set up just around the corner. In fact I had mistakenly been waiting at the wrong place. I went around the corner and stood and watched as the crew began to arrive.

Naoko Mori, who played Toshiko in Torchwood, turned up while it was still very quiet and proceeded to take a video camera out of her bag and began filming the base. She went to the caterers to get some waves and pointed the camera toward me. I wasn't sure if I was supposed to wave or not, and can't remember if I did. I thought nothing of it that she was filming but later on, after transmission I discovered that that day had been her very last on the set of Torchwood, as she was written out at the end of the series. (She was so missed from the show.)

The 2nd AD turned up, said hello and told me to grab some breakfast before I went to costume. As I stood in the queue, a small group of lads came over from the Doctor Who side to steal our yoghurt but the Torchwood crew shooed them away. It turned out that the cocky little lads were playing Sontarans and had had a few days on set. (Remember what I said about regulars getting cocky.)

I went into costume first and was given James' outfit. It was a shame no one was there to take my photo in it as it was a pretty cool costume.

I then went back to my lonely bus, where I quickly took a snap of myself and had just put the camera away when the runner came up to see if I was ready for make-up.

I followed her to the make-up truck and the first thing they did, as usual, was to ask me to shave my beard off! I agreed and had a bit of a hair cut and then went back into the bus to await further instructions.

About an hour later, after I had had several cups of coffee and a serious amount of biscuits, I was called into the studio. It was back in the Torchwood Hub, the main set for the show.

I got to set and props handed me a belt with a sword to complete the costume, although as it turned out, I was never really seen either from the front or from the waist down.

The director spoke to me and explained what was going to happen. The scene was simple enough, a reverse from James's Character, Captain John, was facing John Barrowman's character, Captain Jack.

Extra Time

I had to watch the scene over and over so that I could match exactly not only the movements of the character but also his body movements and how he flowed. (OK, relax, I'm not trying to make out that I can act or anything.

After I felt confident that I'd got it, I went onto the set. John Barrowman was already standing there.

John B introduced himself to me. It went something like this:

JB.   Hello, I'm John

JRW.   Hello John, I'm John

JB   Well John, You know you're playing Captain John Don't you?

JRW   Yes sir. We've actually met before you know. I was John the Double last season.

JB   Oh, Dead Guy! Hello.

JRW   You were telling me all about 'tea-bagging'

JB   Yeah, that's right. Have you tried it yet?

At that, I was so embarrassed that I was actually lost for words. A simple no would have done, I'm sure.

We did the scene several times from several angles using a multitude of lenses. It's quite funny when I watch it now, seeing Captain Jack touching a button on his watch, causing a body drawer to open with a cool bleeping sound effect. In real life when JB touched his watch there were no sounds and two crew members trying to hide behind the fiberglass and timber walls pushed the body drawer slowly out under the watchful eye of the camera crew. Plus, there was no body in it when I was there, as it was filmed on the reverse.

The director got brave with the shots and even got me to turn towards the camera a touch, just to get my cheekbones in.

At the end of the scene I had to kiss JB on the cheek, as Captain John says his goodbyes. We had already tried to get this scene right several times, when JB then turned to me and said politely, "John, when you kiss me, can you make it linger a little longer?" I smiled and replied "only because you'll enjoy it John!"

He didn't find this funny at all. Whoops. He said "Not because I'll enjoy it, that's the way James played it, it's the way the scene needs to be played"

I went bright red. I'm going right red now just thinking about it. I was so embarrassed. JB and I were standing face to face in the small circle that is the autopsy area and all the crew were around us looking down from the balcony area. I'd got too comfortable and had forgotten that extras are not there to be funny.

Another lesson learnt.

We completed the scene and it turned out that that was a wrap on JB for Series 2 of Torchwood (his final scenes). John then spent the next fifteen minutes signing autographs for the crew.

I had just made it into the series as it was being wrapped but for two years in a row I had doubled for the actors but still had yet to be an extra in the series.

Thursday 6th December 2007 -
Doctor Who: Turn Left, (Man in Pub)

This was to be my final time on Doctor Who during the David Tennant era and he wasn't even there that night.

It was a night shift which is always great as I don't need to get time off work, but this particular night must have been the wettest in the history of filming ever.

We were on location in Cardiff at a real pub and Graeme Harper was directing yet again.

It was one of those days when there were lots and lots of extras. I hadn't even noticed that Catherine Tate was on set. I was hoping to see Billie Piper, as rumour had it that she was coming back to the show for a bit.

The scene we were doing was an alternate version of an event that had taken place in the Christmas Special, The Runaway Bride, so at least the weather was a little more realistic than it often is. Usually the Christmas episodes are filmed in the summer months.

The pub was packed with people and there were lots of paparazzi and autograph hunters outside. Catherine Tate was lovely. She invited the autograph hunters inside in the dry and signed and posed for photos for them, so that they didn't have to wait in the rain much longer. She explained that David wasn't coming today, which I wouldn't have known if I hadn't been eavesdropping.

Costume wanted us all in bright colours but smartly dressed and for once, I got to keep my beard. The first half of the night was spent doing background, pretending to drink and sing while the action was a conversation at a corner table with Catherine and some guest actors.

After lunch the cameras moved around to where we were standing. I had been allocated a TV wife and we were chatting away when a man came rushing into the pub, past us shouting to everybody, "There's something in the sky, a giant star," or some such line.

We had to act as if he was either drunk or having a bit of fun as none of us believed him. Then we were to follow him outside to see what he was talking about.

Outside, the paparazzi were still there and we were asked not to speak to them or pose for any photographs. Not that it would have been a scoop or a spoiler, as we were all in normal clothes, looking at something that wasn't there.

A crane had been set up outside with a yellow spot place next to the lens for our first eye line. We came running out of the pub for the brief moment that the rain had stopped and looked dumbfounded at the spot, before finding a new position at the edge of the pub. My friends tell me that dumbfounded is the only facial expression that I have, whether I'm supposed to be happy, sad, lost or actually dumbfounded!

The rain started again, and this time it was serious rain and we were all sent inside. Just so we are clear, no one was worrying about the extras. The costumes were the priority. They couldn't be allowed to get wet, for continuity reasons.

The next shot was set up so that we could watch the giant star-shaped spaceship going around the corner. We were given umbrellas and rehearsed the scene with a ball on the end of a big stick as our eye line.

As soon as the rain slowed little, we took the umbrellas down as fast as we could with several crew members running in between us taking them out of shot. As soon as the umbrellas were clear we did the take.

At one point it rained so hard during a take that we had to cut it early and the umbrellas were quickly given back out but time was short and we couldn't go back inside the pub to keep dry until the shot was in the can.

Catherine Tate joined me under my umbrella as I shared it between about four people. I think it was the first time she had ever spoken to me on set. As I've said before she's not in the least bit rude, she's just a private and quiet person. You kind of get the vibe when actors don't like extras, and this was certainly not one of those cases.

Finally they got what they wanted with all the angles and lens and so we were able to go back inside for a bit. The poor crew on the other hand were already soaked right through but had to carry on working hard outside in the downpour.

When they were ready, we were brought out to film the next part of the scene, in which we went right around the pub and into the road to stand and watch as the Star Spaceship went into the distance and fired upon London. (Yes, I know it was Cardiff really).

Again we had to do it in stages as the rain started and stopped. It was quite a fun scene as we got to do more dumbfounded looks and when the 1st AD shouted, "Now," we had to run backwards and forwards wiping the camera as it went in close on the lead actors.

A wipe is simply walking or running very close to camera. You can wipe several times in a single shot as you're so close to the camera that you're just a black shape going past. People don't tend consciously to notice wipes but it adds a sense of movement to a scene.

Sometimes when there are not enough extras to fill up a space, a couple of people will be kept very close to camera so they can wipe several times and do the same on all angles so it looks like a lot of people walking past.

That was about it for my final David Tennant episode and as it turned out, my final episode for a good few years.

Tuesday 11th December 2007 – Shameless (Rapist)

I had had a call about a month before this job to say that there was a casting for a tiny role, but a speaking one, in Shameless. Unfortunately the casting was on the Friday of that same week, (it was a Wednesday when I got the call), and I was not able to get the time off work.

The Booker from the agency called back again about thirty minutes later and said that the director would really like to meet me, so would I be able to go for a casting a day early, on the Thursday of that week. Again I apologised and said that due to work constraints I couldn't go. I've not really spoken about the great jobs that I have had to turn down, due to not being able to get out of work, including a twelve week job in Milan and Rome. My boss at Morrison's was brilliant, but when I had booked a location, crew and actors and the rest for a training film shoot, that had to take priority.

So I sat at home and carried on working. When he called back again a little while later, saying that the director would really like to see me and could I pop up to the studio that day and meet him after work, I couldn't turn him down.

Later that day, I drove up to Manchester, to the Shameless studios. It was lucky that I was early, as it was one of those places that you would never find, unless you knew what you were looking for, well hidden as it is behind a large black gate! I had to go to a neighbouring building and ask the receptionist if she knew where the Shameless studio was based.

"It's right there in front of us" she said. I felt rather silly, but the gates were shut, so it wasn't at all obvious.

I parked up on the road, (unaware that they have a nice big car park), and made my way to the daunting gate.

I rang the bell and spoke to security, who couldn't have been nicer, and I was taken to meet someone, who told me that the show was running a little behind so would I mind waiting? (I was given coffee and biscuits, so no worries there).

About an hour later, Paul the director came in to see me. He told me my lines and we did the casting. I was supposed to be being arrested, shouting, "Fuck off you wankers!"

I gave it my best shot, but Paul was concerned that my first go was a little camp, so I tried it a few more times and Paul told me there and then that I had got the part.

A few days later I got a call from the agency again telling me the same news and I pretended that it was a surprise.

So, on the day I drove to the big black gates, which were open this time and told security who I was. He showed me where to park and explained where the extras sit. Remember, extras don't get acting roles; we get "walk-ons," which is the proper term for a featured role. Some extras like to think that featured roles are acting roles as it makes them sound better, but the chances are that they'll not get an acting contract, or a credit!

I went to the extras room but everyone was already on set so I sat there patiently with my book.

An hour or so later I was met by the 1st AD who had come in to say hello and to tell me that I wasn't going to be used for a while yet. I was used to that, but nonetheless it was nice of him to pop by.

I carried on reading until I was called into costume. I was to be a sweaty, dirty rapist with egg down my T-shirt and a scratch on my face. I forgot to ask whom I'd attacked.

The make-up girl was amazing. The scratch she applied looked so real, and it didn't take her long to do it either.

Then a young woman came up to me, (I'm ashamed that I have forgotten her name), and said that she was running on the show this week, and that she'd been sent to look after me while I was there.

I had no idea what to do next. I didn't need looking after. She asked if I would like a coffee and I told her that I was happy to make my own, as I like it strong. She kept insisting. She then asked if I'd like to wait in my dressing room and she would bring the coffee in. I pointed out that I didn't have a dressing room. I was just an extra, so I was based in the extras' green room

We finally agreed to go outside to the coffee making facilities and both make drinks together. I really didn't know what I was supposed to do with her, as it would have been rude to go back to reading my book.

We went to watch filming. I had only seen the first couple of series on TV, (This was series five), and had liked the show, so it was nice to watch it being filmed.

We also went for a stroll around the set and inside the garden of the main characters' house.

I met several of the actors, who all seemed really down to earth, as were the regular extras. It breaks my heart saying this, as a proud southerner, but northern extras are not like the majority of southern extras. Northern extras know that they are only extras, don't have a superiority complex about being anything other than extras, and are happy to be called extras as long as the work comes in - although they get a lot less money than their southern colleagues.

Finally I was asked to come on set and was shown my character's house which, like most TV houses, was just a hollow shell.

They wanted to rehearse the scene, so I had few minutes to get into character – at least, as much in character as any extra can be. As the scene was very small, we rehearsed it without the two policemen who were going to arrest me, and it was decided to cut the line in half to simply, "Fuck off". How proud my parents must be!

When they had decided on the camera angle the policemen were brought in and we went straight for a take.

The director wasn't overly pleased with something so we went into Take Two.

Again, the director wanted something more from me.

"How hard can two little words be?"

I asked the extra who was playing the policeman who had hold of me, to really twist my arm, as we came out of the house, and to make sure he really hurt me. He did a very good job of twisting it and I had no difficulty in shouting "Fuck Off!" in a very convincing way. Within moments I was wrapped and the crew were off for the next scene.

2008

A funny thing happened to me on Emmerdale. By now I had been doing background as a Doctor on Emmerdale for a while and had been given my own badge with my own picture on it. That in itself is funny as most of the time the extras are given any old badge with anyone on it if they're just in for a day or two. Sometimes it's not even the right skin colour or even the correct sex.

I won't say I was a regular on Emmerdale, as the producers didn't care which extras turned up, it was just the booker who kept me coming back on, every time there was a hospital scene. Well on this particular day, costume were handing out the badges out, and anyone who remotely resembled the photo on a badge got that badge.

My badge with my actual photo on it was given to someone else. It was decided that this particular someone else looked more like me than I did!

When I asked if I could swap the random badge that I had been given, she still didn't believe that it was me in the photo on the other badge!

Monday 28th January 2008 - Hollyoaks (Doctor)

I have said before that this is the only job in the world with no career prospects. For that matter, anyone who is hoping to build a career in the film industry should avoid becoming an extra at all cost. Once you have been an extra, then it is often the case that no-one in the industry will take you seriously in terms of any other jobs either in front of or behind the camera.

I knew this but didn't care, as I was earning a nice wage and had a brilliant job outside of my extras work that I loved and appreciated everyday.

But even though there are no job prospects as an extra, as your agency booker gets to know who you are and what you are capable of, you can start to get better jobs, with bigger roles, more lines, and so on!

Well, one day, my northern agency booker suddenly upped and left! At a stroke the agency had no idea who I was or what I could do; and for that matter didn't like the fact that I lived so far away from Manchester, Leeds or Liverpool which was where most of the work was!

I used to get offered work every week but all it tended to be was Waterloo Road, for which the studio would ask for us by name; or playing doctors because they knew I had been doing that on Emmerdale for a while.

Extra Time

There is a unwritten rule in the north that if you're in the Rovers Return on Coronation Street then you are not allowed to be in the Woolpack on Emmerdale and vice versa. It's one or the other and yet I was suddenly a Doctor on Emmerdale, Hollyoaks and Coronation Street all around the same time.

On this particular day on Hollyoaks, there were a bunch of extras, who had all won their roles by bidding in a charity auction. There were only three real extras to film a hospital scene and then to go outside to do some passing by.

The 'auction' extras wanted to talk to us and ask us what other shows we had done. They were very excited and thought this must be great fun, which it is most of the time, but they wanted to know what it was like to be a real extra. We explained that we tend to keep ourselves to ourselves and don't speak to actors unless spoken to especially on this show as most of the actors on Hollyoaks would never speak to the extras.

Except that that day the actors were all over the auction bidders, posing for photos with them in the studio and outside, while the three of us just sat there, invisible. Even the 3rd AD came up to us and apologised, as he said, those particular actors didn't even talk to him usually.

Wednesday 13th February 2008 –

Bonekickers - 18th Century British Soldier

This was a night shoot in Bristol and it was a seriously cold night. We had to get there quite early in the afternoon, as there were quite a few of us, all dressed up and all bewigged. We had been for a fitting a few days before so that everyone was ready, but it still took a while. We couldn't get breakfast until we had been to costume and make-up.

TV has strange working hours, so we are never surprised to be eating breakfast at any time of the day.

A new girl was doing my hair, so things took a little longer and I was becoming quite upset seeing all the other extras coming in and going out to eat while I was still sitting there, having my hair very slowly curled.

In the end another hairdresser came along and finished the job for her and I just managed to get my breakfast before we had to go on the minibus to the location.

The scene was set during the American War of Independence and involved lots of American soldiers, a number of black slaves and just a few of us British soldiers.

I would have liked to have put on my Long johns but the costume I was wearing had short legs, so I wouldn't have been able to get away with it. On the whole I considered myself lucky however, because the poor black guys had to have bare legs and nothing on their feet. It was starting to ice up outside!

Extra Time

After we dropped our bags off in the extras' green room we were sent outside to have musket training – another of the many weapons that I have had to learn to use since becoming an extra.

The director James Strong came over to see us. I had met him on Doctor Who. His Christmas episode, Voyage of the Damned, which had featured Kylie Minogue, had broken all records for viewing figures.

As a Doctor Who fan, I had to say hi and congratulate him on the Christmas special. I love his work and it was a great pleasure to be on his set again. Call me what you will and I'm sorry if I'm now coming over as one of those boring, ass-kissing extras, but I'm always going to be keen to express my appreciation when I'm on something science fiction related!

After gun training we were sent to set to get some shots in before it got dark. We British soldiers were being ambushed. One guy had to have a fight with a stunt man so he got some training prior to the take.

I was the first to be killed, shot in the back and falling forwards as if the bullet had passed right through me. The floor was a stony path, which hurt like mad; but to be fair, it's not often we get so much action, so no one minded a few cuts and scratches.

After I was shot and the other three chaps were also dead, one of the 'Americans' was to stab me in the gut to finish me off. I'd always wanted to do the "being finished off" bit where lifting my legs and arms in one final breath of life. I'm proud to say that the actor finishing me off had been the lead in the London theatre run of the Lion King! If you're going to be killed, be killed by someone cool! The bad guys then had to rob our corpses of our guns.

Unfortunately, my gun had become caught in my wig. He kept pulling and pulling at it and I was trying to be dead while at the same time not letting him move the gun. It would have taken all night to get that bloody hair back on.

Luckily they called cut and the hair stayed. My killer had noticed the problem, and for his part, was not trying too hard to get the gun.

The final shot before it got dark was to be a close-up of me, being shot. I was going to be squibbed (a squib is an electronic gun shot on either a person or object).

It was a race against time. At one point I had seven people around me. My trousers were around my knees and my jacket was open. I was having wires put down my trousers and out the bottom, that would be attached to the Visual Effects box; the costume people were cutting a hole in my jacket for the rip to open and attaching a blood filed rubber with an explosive to the inside; meanwhile make-up were doing my hair and powdering my face. This was all happening at the same time!

I liked the attention to be honest. Who wouldn't?

Extra Time

The scene was easy. An 'American soldier' would fire his musket; the camera would pull focus from him to me and one step, two step, bang! I would look surprised and fall out of frame!

There could only be one take at this as the light was fading fast. There wasn't even time for a rehearsal.

You can feel a squib going off, it's no more than like just being lightly tapped, so I knew that it had gone off early. "Action! - Bang, One step" and the squib went off. Realising what had happened, I fell.

James Strong went mad! What was that? It was supposed to happen on the second step. Luckily he didn't seem to be shouting at me, so I figured I had done what I was supposed to, however the camera hadn't pulled focus in time and the shot had been lost.

James shouted to everyone to set me up again so suddenly I had about seven people all over me and I just stood there with my trousers around my ankles while the costume was cleaned and sewn up; SFX put a new squib on me and wired it; and make-up cleaned me up after my face first fall onto the floor. (Stunts had given me knee pads this time).

They all worked as fast as they could but the light was nigh on gone and the camera crew couldn't hold out much longer.

Just as I was ready for the retake, James called "Lunch!" We had run out of light!

Special Effects came back over to take the new squib out. "He's not happy with you" I was told.

"Me?" I replied in shock. "This is all my fault?"

"Yes, you fell at the wrong time and they missed the shot"

I was devastated. When any crew member says something to an extra, then it must be true!

I got my lunch and went onto the dining bus. There was my directing hero sitting at a table with the director of photography, looking moody as hell.

I went up to him and said "I'm so sorry about that".

He just looked at me and said unconvincingly "It's okay".

I was so upset. How could I have let down a brilliant Doctor Who director? This isn't a cool job after all, when things like that can happen. Don't work with your idols!

After lunch The Americans were being used and we Brits had nothing to do but wait in the warm, which was rather nice, as it had got seriously cold now that it was dark.

Later, we were called so that we could be shot again, although we were supposed to be different soldiers than earlier, and this was more of a silhouette shot.

I asked the 1st AD if we were being squibbed up for this one and he said no, as we were being shot in the back and there wasn't time.

I told him how glad I was, after I had messed the earlier one up.

Extra Time

"You didn't mess it up", he said.

I told him that Special effects had told me I had.

"Are you kidding? They messed it up by setting off the squib too early".

It was just as I had thought. I hadn't let James Strong down at all! All was better in the world and I loved this job again.

Well, we all tried really hard to get the scene complete first time as it was a tad chilly and the crew were running behind, so we were given numbers one to four. I was to go down on the first shot, on the second shot it was the next guy's turn and so on.
We did as we were told and played dead lying in the frozen grass for ages. It was tough holding my breath after walking and falling down. Usually when I'm dead, I start off dead.

We managed it and were sent back again to warm up until we were needed again.

It was getting late before I was finally called back out for a fight scene with explosions and everything, but I had to remain close to camera, dead lying over metal cannon, for the whole sequence.

I was standing there waiting to go outside onto set and starting to shake with the cold. My teeth were rattling. All of a sudden I felt someone put their hand down my backside, I turned and it was the costume lady, putting a warmer thing down the base of my spine to warm me up.

It didn't help much, but soon afterwards I was put into place. The cannon was so unbelievably cold that I was surprised that my face didn't freeze to it.

I lay there and although I knew that there was going to be an explosion and when it was going to go off, I still found myself jumping every time.

That wasn't why I was sent back in though. I was so cold that my whole body was shaking and there was nothing I could do to stop it. Not ideal when you're supposed to be dead!

So, I was sent indoors, to be replaced by Kristian. He was pleased! (Sorry Kristian to leave you out in the cold sir!).

That was about it for Bonekickers, which was one of the few shows that I have been in that I watched on TV. It was a show that was hated by the critics and became known as one of those shows that was so bad, it became funny, but I actually really liked it. Every episode started well and was great until about three quarters of the way through; but then went off into some stupid climax. For me, being a West Country guy, it was great to see my home town on Television.

Sunday 24th February 2008 –

Barclays Bank Corporate film, Customer

This wasn't the most interesting job in the world but it was a night shoot in Coventry. I had been back in London all weekend so this was on the way home and I was working the next day!

I drove straight to set and having already had little sleep all weekend I stopped pretty much outside the bank, being a Sunday night I could park anywhere, and settled down for a little sleep in the car prior to starting work.

Extra Time

My alarm went off and I went to the door, I was sent upstairs with the other extras, several of whom I knew. They had all been working on Doctor Who so I ended up knowing lots of 'spoilers' that I didn't want to. I know that many Doctor Who fans dream about having insider knowledge about what is coming up on the show and do everything they can to uncover secrets, but I never look at stuff in magazines or on the internet about future episodes as I don't like to ruin the show for myself. However, not only am I forever finding out stuff when I am on the Doctor Who set myself, but other extras, who know I love the show so much, are forever telling me more than I'd like to know.

This 'corporate' was being filmed in two parts. The first was simply someone walking into a branch to find it a complete mess; while in the other version it is how the store should be at all times, so it was to be a brilliant version of the same scenes.

I figured this shouldn't take long. I made 'Corporates" for a living, and knew that I could have had it all finished within five hours or so.

How wrong could I have been? It took ages and ages. All the while I was struggling to stay awake. My character was supposed to be a bored customer sitting waiting to be seen, but not getting anywhere. Now that's a tough role in a warm stuffy, comfortable, quiet set. So of course I fell asleep.

When I awoke an hour or so later, the crew were filming on the other side of the room. I asked someone if I was still needed in the seat where they had put me. He said no, and then told me that they had loved the fact that I was actually asleep and had filmed me!

Fancy that? I was being paid to sleep!

The filming went on longer than expected and the crew asked us if we'd like to stay for more money. So on that note, I said my goodbyes and went home! I really didn't do this for the money and no money was worth staying awake any longer that night.

Meanwhile at work with my real job, it was time to get my new company car, so I got the booklet and spent ages on the internet looking up all the available models. I finally chose a black diesel hatchback 2008 Ford Mondeo and put the order in. It would be a few months before I got it.

Wednesday 2nd April 2008 - The Cup - Parent

This Mocumentary (fake documentary) was filmed in Manchester. I played one of a group of parents of a kids' football team, who were playing the actors' team and would lose.

The difference with this show was that they wanted a documentary feel to it, as if a camera team were on the pitch with the teams (which they were), so it didn't matter if we looked into the lens, something that we are taught never to do as a rule. If someone on screen looks into the camera, they are in effect, looking right into the eyes of the audience, and so making them aware that they're watching a TV programme. This doesn't apply, of course, with a POV shot, which is supposed to give the view as seen by one of the characters.

Anyway, back to the job in hand. It was a really windy day. We had to put a tent up so that the camera crew could film us and it took ages. I took control of the situation by reading out the instructions. This wasn't because I wanted to appear in charge but more to do with the fact that I couldn't put a tent up to save my life! It must have been very amusing for all the crew and the actors, who got to watch a bunch of extras trying to put this tent up.

By lunch time the tent was starting to bend in the wind and pipes were snapping off and breaking. We decided it safest to keep out of it!

One of the Footballing kids had made the decision that I was going to be his TV dad and I was to call his name every time he got the ball. This seemed like fun at first but as it was TV and the scenes were all well rehearsed I don't think he ever touched the ball!

It was quite a short day as documentary style TV shows are far quicker as there are not usually different angles or lens types and lighting is very basic.

I don't know if this show got aired. I never heard of it again.

Saturday 5th April – Friday 11th April 2008 –

Casualty – Man who looks like Rik Mayall

I got my usual costume call from Casualty and was told to bring some late summer clothes. I was to be a patient in the hospital, bad news as all patients on the show do is walk around in circles for a week.

When I arrived, the costume Department had had a brainstorm. They wanted to have some fun and get Casualty on "TV Burp" (which wasn't on at the time of year this episode was to be aired).

They wanted 4 people to look like the "Young Ones" and one to look like "Harry Hill"

I became Rik. The guy playing Harry Hill, whom I found out was called Soni was to become a great friend of mine.

We were given stuff to wear in the end but we got the feeling that the Young Ones thing was Costume's idea alone and that the rest of the crew and the cast were completely in the dark about it.

Costume had told us that in the old days they used to have some fun on the show and once they even had a man in a wet suit sitting in the waiting room waiting for help.

When we were taken to set, the 3rd AD didn't once put us all together, but I was placed at the counter as if I was waiting for the receptionist to talk to me.

The costume guy had told me to do my full Rik Mayall impression! I did as requested (extras are not to reason why) and thrust my groin out with my hands at my hips and stroked the side of my head when I mimed to the receptionist all the while bringing my top lip as high as I could.

The action was going on next to me and I was in the background giving it my all.

When it came to the next scene, I was asked to act normally and then we assumed everyone had caught on but thought it was a bad idea because we had brought too much attention to ourselves and thus the 3rd AD wasn't able to double us as well as he could if we had simply been standing there looking bland.

I went from doing my best Rik Mayall impression to being as normal and unobtrusive as possible within an hour and we still had a whole week to do on this show!

Most TV shows don't mind if the extras fall asleep between scenes as some days we're not used at all but Casualty has a serious issue with extras if they do fall asleep. Your agency is called and you're taken off the show never to come back.

Different people have different views on this. Some say that you are being paid to be there and if you were to fall asleep on a real job you would get the sack. Whilst others say that you're not doing anything so what harm is there if you have a sleep, especially if you have driven in everyday and got up at some stupid time in the morning in order to look awake whilst in a shot!

I'll let you make your own mind up on this subject.

One of the people I spent the week with was a young lady called Sian who was a booker for a modeling agency. I had told her about my job writing, casting, scouting for locations, shooting and editing corporate films. I mention her because she will crop up again later in this story and become one of the catalysts that changed my life without even knowing it.

We happened to be staying in the same Bed and Breakfast and she convinced me to keep my door locked, teasing me that the old lady who owned the house would come into my room at night!

This was a brilliant fun week as most of us went out together most nights after work.

One of the things that makes this job worth doing is the other extras you're working with. When you get a great bunch together it can be so funny. It's also weird how you can get so friendly with people and yet after you finish working with them you don't see them again until the next job if ever again.

Extras also don't take offence when we forget each other's names and how we know each other because there are simply so many of us and we do so many jobs.

Sunday 27th April 2008 – Sunshine – Second hand Car dealer

This was a random TV show filmed near Manchester and staring Steve Coogan. I had been booked for a featured role but I hadn't needed to cast for it, I just seemed to get it!

It was a brilliantly sunny day and I drove to a small village south of Manchester and found the car park that had become the base of operations

I met with the 2nd AD who had booked me and she asked me to stand by in the extras bus. I went up to the bus which was deserted as everyone else was on set.

Extra Time

Now would be a good time for a sleep I decided, settling down in the back of the bus, to be woken at lunch time by a whole bunch of people. Like a good extra, I went to get my lunch and brought it back onto the bus.

As I ate I noticed that Steve Coogan himself was sitting at the next table eating with some extras! Of course, I listened in as he explained that there was a time when he wouldn't think of sitting on the extras' bus and talking to the extras but that he'd rather eat here than in his trailer on his own.

I decided that I liked him. I'd never actually seen any of his films, but he seemed okay to me.

This was lucky as it turned out as later on I had to work with him, just the two of us!

After lunch, everyone went back to work and left me alone again apart from the costume people, who came to see me to decide on two outfits to turn me into a cheap second hand car dealer.

Steve Coogan was driven to set while I went down in the minibus on my own (which made me feel slightly special). I've told you before that extras like to be made to feel special.

We were filming at a local sales garage and the prop car had been placed out front. Literally hundreds of people had come out to watch the filming. It seemed as if the whole village was out to see their town made famous.

In the first scene Steve Coogan was selling me his car. He introduced himself and that was pretty much all that was ever actually said to me before we started filming.

The car was set up and we stood side by side while I was given a few hundred pounds to count out and give to Steve, whose character was down on his luck and needed the money. I never saw a script for this scene, so it was all pretty much ad-libbed.

I had always thought that I'd be nervous; trying to act in front of a real actor but it was surprisingly easy as I guess there was no acting required.

The scene didn't take long to film and when it was completed, Steve was driven back to Base for a change of clothes. I of course had to change in the dirty office of the garage!

I went to get a cup of coffee from the on-set coffee facilities when suddenly this weird thing happened. People started waving at me out of the windows of their homes and staring at me in the street.

Then a man with a young girl came up to me saying, "My daughter knows you from TV, What have you been in?"

"Trust me, you won't know me, I'm just a no body" I replied.

He wouldn't let it go. "No really, my daughter says she knows you from TV, What have you been in?"

"Well I've been in lots of things, Coronation Street, Doctor Who, Hollyoaks"

"You were in Doctor Who? Which one?"

"Look I'm just an extra. You won't have seen me."

They finally left, still believing that I was some sort of actor.

Extra Time

It was a weird feeling. I almost felt guilty having my cigarette in public, as if I had to be some sort of role model for the afternoon.

For the next scene I had to sell Steve Coogan's character a car. It wasn't much, just a handshake and , "Thanks for the business guv," or something like that. And that was it. Steve Coogan vanished and I never saw him again. I was taken back to base (not before all the prop cash was counted back in) and I was wrapped.

As usual I never got around to seeing this show, but it was turned out that I was in two different episodes. My friend texted me to tell me that she had seen me in it but that my lines had been cut! Typical but anyway, not to worry as I still get paid the same.

Chapter 2

Everything Changes

At this point I loved my life. I had a great job with a nice car. Money wasn't an issue. I had a nice house and so on.

I had just been given my Twenty Year award with Morrisons, I had just come back from my annual holiday to New York with my friends and I had booked to spend two weeks in Cannes for the film festival.

I had turned down a promotion at work because it would have meant being in the office all week and moving to Bradford. If I was ever to move again, then I wanted to go back to the South West.

At a level way above my lowly station however, moves were afoot that would change everything. Sir Ken Morrison had left Morrison's and the new CEO was apparently keen to put his mark on the company, so we were being restructured. My job was going to be safe as there were still going to be in-house corporate films and I would still be working for the same team, who knew what I was capable of.

Just before setting off for Cannes I had an e-mail from my boss asking me to pop in on the Thursday after I got back "for a chat and a catch up".

The trip was brilliant and I was looking forward to coming back to work. I had just completed a Fish Counter film that had to be done twice due to a major policy change while the first version was still in edit so once that was released I would be free to start the next two projects.

I put my best suit on and went to Bradford to see my boss as requested, only to be met by the Personnel Department. I imagined that I was going to be asked to slip a job in for them as I had recently completed for them an audio version of the staff handbook for the hard of hearing.

We went to a pre booked office and sat down. I guess I should have been suspicious by now but it came as a total shock when my boss told me that the in-house Corporate Films Department was no longer needed and that the company was doing so well now that they could afford to have all their films made externally without the hassle of keeping me within the business.

I was offered more training work, signing off assistant managers for the stores but I had always said to myself that if this day ever came I would leave and go into business on my own making corporate films for other businesses at a reasonable rate.

Part of my decision was that I was enjoying working as an extra so much and I didn't want to have to give that up. I look back now and realize that this was one of the biggest mistakes of my life. I'll never earn that sort of money again and I'll never have the job security and the perks that go with that.

I think it surprised them when I asked if redundancy was on the table (or maybe it was what they wanted. I'll never know).

I was offered a rubbish package and put on three months garden leave with immediate effect. Everything had to be returned within the week: my camera and film equipment; my car; my mobile phone and my head-office pass. I lost my Bupa care, my pension stopped and my SAYE accounts were closed. Ouch!

The first thing I had to do was find a car. I went to every garage I could and asked specifically for a small black diesel car for under £3000. I ended up buying a 2003 Rover, which was a tad old but for that price I took it, as the money would not last long!

I began spending time living with my friends in London and I joined more Extras agencies. I didn't want to be a full time extra but it was a way to make ends meet until my video business took off. I was also keen to get into something that I hadn't done before, behind the scenes work on TV shows and films. I'd love to AD a film myself one day.

Monday 26th May 2008 – Britain's Got the Pop Factor - Fan

This was a TV comedy show based on the X Factor, directed by and starring Peter Kay (who had been in Doctor Who!)

It was a bank holiday Monday job which was quite rare and a night shoot. We had to meet up in a big car park in Manchester where they had set up an extras base. There were loads of us.

We got there and had lunch as soon as we turned up, the producers having decided that the best way to save money was to feed us first so that they wouldn't have to bother later on, and to sign and collect our chits (extras signing out forms) as soon as we arrived to save on doing it all after the shoot.

Extra Time

This didn't turn out to be the greatest idea. Extras were going home by the minute having realized that as they were now signed out there was nothing to make them stay, but they would still receive the money for working all night.

I had no intention of going home. It didn't even cross my mind. I needed the work so badly that I wouldn't dream of getting sacked and losing an agency just because I could skip work for a night.

The minibuses picked us all up and we headed to Granada studios. We thought we were going onto the Coronation Street set, as this is in the centre of Granada Studios but we walked right past the Street set to a new part of the studio that I'd never worked in before. It was an outside set that was made to look like a movie première complete with red carpet and waist-high fences.

The job in hand was that we had to scream and shout for bands as if we knew who they were. They were supposed to be some sort of X-Factor winners that we loved.

When that scene was completed we were herded around the corner to another very similar set up which, I think, was supposed to be the after party. Again it was a case of screaming when they called action.

It was nothing too strenuous and Peter Kay was really nice to the crowds although it was weird being directed by a man dressed as a woman! As the star of the show Peter was in drag as 'Geraldine' and so had to direct in costume.

Friday 13th June 2008 – Doctors - Race Announcer

I spent a lot of my time just doing Coronation Street, Emmerdale and Waterloo Road but then I got a show that everyone in the world had done except me. Doctors

I had been booked as a speaking role and would receive the script when I get there. I don't know why, after 10 years of doing Background work I was suddenly quite scared. I didn't know where to park, where to sign in or where to wait so I called upon Sian (Who I had met at Casualty)

She talked me through it as I had always gotten lost in Birmingham as a whole but had found this place with the help of the Sat Nav! (If only these had always been around)

I parked up and sat in the car for a while before getting brave and going in.

I don't know why it is that I worry so much when it's my first time on a show that is always based in the same place whereas I don't worry when I go to locations. It's something about not wanting to look stupid by not knowing the rules.

It was all fine and I was shown the extras' green room. I was alone as the rest of the extras with my unit were already on set as they had an earlier call time.

I was given the script and it was quite a lot but all simple stuff like starting a race and calling out who the winner was.

They gave me some cool props like the stop watch!

I read through my lines and was then asked to wait at the reception until the minibus was ready to take me to location.

Extra Time

I had never seen an episode of Doctors (and to my shame still haven't) so I didn't know who were actors/extras or guests but it didn't seem to matter on this show as everyone seemed very down to earth.

I was finally taken to location but when I got there it turned out that the 1st AD wanted to announce the race!

I said nothing and obviously no-one had said anything to him about me (either that or he didn't care)

I did stand there and pretend to be timing the race though as I wasn't going to let my super fun prop out of my hands!

What made things worse were the fact that after lunch we had to do the end of the race and the 1st AD started moaning that he's got to get back in front of the camera again! Poor thing. I ended up with less money as I didn't have that featured role after all. (We never look forward to the money until the chit has been signed at the end of the day, as it doesn't matter what we've been booked to do, we only get paid for what we actually do which can be something completely different.)

Sian, as I mentioned earlier worked for a modelling agency in Birmingham and they had been asked to cast for a commercial but weren't too sure on rates and casting for acting roles so they asked me to pop over and help out for a few days (Sian remembered that I used to do this for Morrison's)

I went down to Birmingham for 2 days to help set up and find suitable applicants for a commercial. This was my first time on the other end of the telephone from a booking office. I didn't remotely enjoy it but the casting itself was fun. I even applied myself but didn't get a role.

But I did get to meet a couple of people who helped change my life! Its weird when small things happen and when you look back on it, it was very important.

I met Steve Bishop and Tony Jopia. Tony was directing this commercial.

Tuesday 1st/Wednesday 2nd July 2008 –

Football Commercial – Fan/passer by/passenger

This is only being put in here to point out that I ended up getting a couple of days paid work from helping to cast it.

Birmingham was doubling for London so they had hired a big red Double Decker bus and on the second day they were still short of extras so we took the bus to town to try and rally up some extras for the afternoon.

Granted that afternoon was spent in a football stadium with a green screen to try and make the whole place look completely full so it wasn't very exciting and the new extras we had got didn't want to stay long and were longer interested in earning any money.

Friday 25th July 2008 – The Sarah Jane Adventures - Teacher

This was a 1950's episode and was filmed in a quaint little village just outside Swansea. It was directed by Mr Graeme Harper again.

I had got into my costume complete with cape and hat and I saw Graeme. "Hello" I called. We were still in the car park that we were using for a base just outside the village.

"Hello" Said Mr Harper. "I have a surprise for you later!"

"What sort of surprise" I asked suspiciously

"You're my last scene of the day and you're going to get very wet" He had amused himself with this line and then walked off into the production trailer.

I was sure this was just a joke as no one had mentioned getting wet before I turned up today.

I then saw a chap from the props department and he said "Oh you're the teacher huh?" "I've spent most of the morning filling your pool up"

He explained to me that was to be sitting over the "Dunk the teacher" pool for most of the day but he wasn't aware if I was to get wet.

Graeme was surly jesting as props would know and costume would have said something.

There was a rumour around that the Doctor was going to be in this episode as a Tardis had been seen around but this turned out not to be true.

Again I had had to remove my beard and this time I had to keep the silly moustache for nearly a week as I was coming back next Wednesday.

The day was sunny and bright and the location was a field in the village made up to look like a 1950's fair.

Everyone got to walk around for scenes except me as I was sitting on my plank above a pool of water. It wasn't rigged up so it was quite safe to sit on.

There were some brilliant characters amongst the extras including one chap who could juggle anything. It wasn't really like work as we sat in the sun all day.

Every time I saw Mr Harper he would say "Last scene of the day!" with a naughty grin on his face. I still didn't really believe him.

It was only later at the penultimate scene that I realised he might not be joking after all.

Extra Time

There was supposed to a storm coming so we have to grab some gear and run inside and we did this a couple of times on rehearsal. It was just before the take when someone came up to me and said "Graeme doesn't want you in this scene"

It twigged straight away then! He doesn't want me in this scene for continuity and I'm supposed to be wet through!

Sure enough, after the scene the whole camera crew started up towards my pool and set up behind me. It did cross my mind that if I'm to get soaked through, it would be nice to have my face in shot but they wanted the kids in shot who throw the balls to make the plank drop.

Props set up my plank so that it would drop as soon as the word was given.

The kids threw the balls at the target and on the third one I was to drop. I was told to go as deep as I could as this would be a one take wonder!

They turned over and the first ball got thrown. It didn't matter if they hit the target or not as it was the prop guy who was letting me drop.

The second ball was thrown and around all the other extras had gathered and were really looking forward to this.

The third ball was thrown and suddenly I'm in the air and falling. I landed with a splash but it wasn't that deep so I only got wet to the waist and it as pretty warm from standing around all day. The extras and crew gave me a nice cheer

The scene was cut and I was whisked away to a tent with the costume girls and started getting undressed. I was half undressed when a crew member came back in and said "They want to do it again"

I put my wet and now a tad cold clothes back on and went back to set and the plank was back in place and the camera crew had moved position around the front. My face would be in it now.

It was exactly the same as before but when I dropped I made sure I fell more onto my back so that the whole costume went under.

I then made sure that I stayed in character and kept a scowl until they cut (Staying in character on Doctor who related programmes is important as they'll be watched and scrutinised for years to come!)

I went back to the tent to change and I kept taking clothes off until I was just in my pants and socks. The costume lady told me to take my socks off and they'll replace them with costume socks so I did as I was told and then she asked if I'd like to take my pants off. This should be a new record – I was in my pants on the set of Dr who and Torchwood and now Sarah Jane!I kindly reused the offer of taking the underwear off and waited until I was back in the costume tent rather than in a field full of crew, cast and extras!

They gave me a dressing gown but unfortunately it was just an old costume one and not an exclusive SJS BBC one so I gave it back once I was dressed.

I never saw my socks again but in the knowledge that I was Sarah Jane's teacher at school – It was worth the sacrifice.

Wednesday 30th July 2008 – Sarah Jane Adventures - Teacher

A week later I was back on the show but this time we were based inside as there was supposed to have been a storm.

The costume department had decided to get around continuity and rather have me soaking wet in my teacher's cape and hat, I was in a suit. It was great as this time I could mosey around the set like everyone else.

On one of the scenes we had tea in a cup and saucer so I simply had to do the thing with the little finger poking out.

It was hot tea on the first take but I guessed they weren't going to have time to refill it so I just pretended to drink it as it was going cols very fast.

It was a weird scene as Anjli Mohindra comes in and she's Asian so we had to look at her as if we'd never seen an Asian before and look her up and down with sour looks on our faces. Anjli was brilliant and I've bumped into her a few times since. I think she's one of the best things to happen to that show.

Liz Sladen didn't say much that day but did warn us all to be careful on the stone steps leading to the location.

It's not often that an internal location was exactly where it was supposed to be in the episode.

I said Hi to Christopher Pizzey who played Sarah Janes Dad. I told him he'd be loved on the convention circuit now and he said that the producers had already told him that he had a very special role.

Friday 8th August 2008 –

The Choir (All the small things) Read-through

Extras don't just do TV work, I used to get a few Read-throughs for other shows. This is when a show is ready to go into production and so all the Head of Departments and Actors are brought together to do a big read through the first block of scripts (Shows are broken down into Blocks in every season which may have different directors or other crew)

I was asked to cover a spot on this particular day as the actor had yet to be cast. It was at the BBC centre in Manchester.

I got to the main gate and they had reserved a parking spot for me (I was told not to tell the security that I'm just an extra replacing an actor)

I then made my way to the front entrance and there was Phil Collinson (ex producer of Doctor who who was now Head of Drama in BBC Manchester)

I knew he must have recognised me as the Doctor who geek that always has to stop him in the street when I see him about to talk Doctor who! He was good enough to not say anything. It was weird as other actors were turning up, people like Clive Rowe and Sarah Lancashire were there and every time they introduced themselves to me thinking I was a fellow actor I found myself saying "I'm just here to replace someone" as I knew they'd not like the fact that I'm an extra.

I spent most of the day with a brilliant chap called Bryan Dick and we talked about jobs and the like but I had forgotten he was an actor and when he told me he had done Torchwood, I didn't think of talking further about it. It was only when I got home that I realised he had played "Adam" - The lead guest actor and title character from an episode in Season 2!

Strangely enough the other replacement for the day was my constant on screen partner Helen. She did an amazing job this day as she was playing about 3 roles and there were times when the whole room was quiet and she would just be reading all these characters lines in different voices.

I on the other hand was rubbish!

I've just ahead, sorry. When all the actors had arrived and everyone was introducing themselves we were asked to go up to a room they had prepared for proper introductions. It had cakes, fruit, cakes, sandwiches and cakes in it. A whole table of delightful delights. I wanted to jump in and eat as much as I could and fill my bag for later like a proper extra. I even waited for the other people to eat first before I got my plate filled. It's things like this that gives extras away who are trying to hide their identities!

We all sat at tables and talked. I couldn't help but mention to Clive Rowe that I had enjoyed his role in the Doctor who Christmas special. I asked if he had had any good feedback about it and he simply shrugged and said "That's why I'm here!"

The downside about read-throughs is that all the actors would have read the script already and for me it was my first time even seeing one!

We gestured into a room with a big table and our names were already written on cards so we knew where to sit. We were given scripts and cast and crew lists as we came in.

I sat down next to Helen at the bottom end of the table. All the HODs (Head of Departments) were sitting around he room.

We all went around the room one by one saying our names and what we do. I just Said I was standing in.

When everyone around the room had finished, Phil Collinson said a few words and off we went with Phil reading narration.

I didn't try to get into character whilst reading, I just read it through at a pace I could cope with but at one point the whole room went quiet. I looked up to see why and everybody was staring at me. I looked back down and turned the page. Oops, they were waiting on me as it was my line next.

At the end of the day, I introduced myself to the Head of "2 Entertain" video and pointed out I'm not an actor (as she may have guessed) and that I was Head of Internal Corporate's From one of the UKs leading retail stores and I would like to be involved in the behind the scenes.

We exchanged e -mails and as you can guess I never heard back from her again.

I did a few of these read-throughs and it was great how the BBC never told my agency how rubbish I was and so my agency kept thinking I was good and kept sending me!

Monday 11th August 2008 – Lewis – Passer-by

More recently I was on a show and the word passer-by had been given a new lease of life as it was called "London Onlooker" It's the whole SA thing all over again!

I was in Oxford and walking to the production office to sign in when I heard a "Oi John" from behind me. I turned around and who should be coming out of his trailer but Bryan Dick! I couldn't believe the coincidence as I had only seen him 2 days ago up in Manchester

I had a chance to tell him I couldn't believe I had not realised he was Adam in Torchwood,!

It was one of those days when the extras were just used to walk up and down the streets close to the main actors so that all the real passer bys could be utilised but a little further away so that it's not noticed if they stare at the camera!

The Lewis teams are good about letting the locals cameo in the show and Kevin Whatley speaks to extras so we like him!

Tuesday 12th August 2008 – Casualty -Gowned Patient

I was just booked as patient/visitor walking around hospital on this day. Nothing out of the ordinary and just another day on set.

I was outside talking to the guest actor about nothing in particular when as usual the conversation about Doctor who came up (It just happens, I do not push for this conversation with every actor)

I said I like the show and he said he was in it.

Suddenly stupid me had yet again failed to recognise him. "Which one were you in?" I asked

"The Big Brother episode" he said

"Oh my lord, you're Jamie Bradley? "And he was shocked I knew his name.

We then discussed the awful night gown he was wearing and I felt comfortable enough to make a little joke about it. (Don't worry he was fine about it)

The break was over and we went back inside. Once in, the costume department called me and said they'd like to change me.

If it hadn't happened so quickly I would have though it was revenge but it was just coincidence. One minute I'm making fun of Jamie in his hospital gown and the next, I'm in the bed next him wearing the same!

He saw the funny side of this too!

Friday 15th August 2008 –

In Love with Barbara – Lots of people

This was filmed as Men are Wonderful and I would have liked to have seen it but the name changed and I wasn't made aware. (It was Tom Burke who told me that much later)

It was a low budget BBC film about the love life of Barbara Cartland.

This was filmed in Bristol and was one of those shoots that was very fast. If one take was fine, rather than do another just in case, they'd just go onto the next shot and shoots like that are brilliant fun as there's no standing about plus we were used in just about every scene.

Our sections were set in the 1950's and we were visitors in museum, passing by outside, fellow MPs and the like.

I had seen a film I loved called "I want Candy" and had recently bought it on DVD. It's such a funny film and I had never met Tom Burke before but was a little excited to see him so I could tell him how much I loved that movie.

Half way through the day I was left on set with him and he finally said hello (You're about to understand why actors don't talk to us) I felt that him saying hello was an invitation to conversation so I said Hello back and followed it with "I loved that film you made, I want Candy!"

I thought he might be pleased that someone loved a movie he starred in so much.

He went mad at me. "I hate that film because I hated ..." (I'll not say why he hated it as that's his business) but I just stood there wishing the ground would open up right where I'm standing.

I think he realised he'd gone a little ballistic and tried to be nice by asking what I do for a living and stuff but the damage was done. We couldn't look at each other in the eye for the rest of the day. It was a new learning curve (There seem to be so many) but never tell an actor how much you enjoyed their film again!

Some good news that day was that I got some dialogue and even though it was low budget they were fair and paid me for it.

Saturday 30th August 2008

Britannia High – Audio Wild track

Again this was is one of those jobs that extras tend to get and it's great because you paid a full day for what is usually just a couple of hours.

A wild track is just background voices or sounds but on this day we had a few specific people to voice too.

There was a character in this short lived show called Lola (Played by Rana Roy) and myself with the other 6 or so extras spent a few hours covering a couple of episodes that included calling her name out so much! We were paps and photographers and they all just had to call her name out." Over here Lola, look at this camera Lola"

We all got to single out people out to dub and it was fun but tough on the throat and all this was done in a recording studio in Manchester.

We then had to walk to the TV studio where they film the show and who should be bump into walking out but poor Rana Roy who didn't know what hit her and we suddenly start shouting "Lola, over here lola, look this way Lola"

Thursday 4th September 2008 – Merlin – Kain's men

September 2008 was a strange time as I had more pencils than I had ever had before. A pencil is when they're not sure if we'll be needed or not so we have to book it in our diary and not take any other work as we're penciled but they don't have to give us work or let us know if we're needed until the night before and we can't have any loss of earning money or cancellation fee because we were only ever penciled. Some agencies let you come off a pencil if you're offered other guaranteed work while others do not and will refuse to find out if you're needed or not. Pencils are the extras worst nightmares and there seems to be getting more of them. (Okay, maybe not the worst Nightmare as I can think of worse ones but we jolly well don't like pencils!)

Anyhow, Merlin was never a pencil. I had 5 days booked. The first was a sword fighting practice day and the others were the actual shoot next week.

This was down in Barry, South Wales. I drove down and had a costume fitted to start with. I didn't get a photo in it as I knew I would be back next week.

There were about 10 of us and we spent the whole day learning basic sword skills and stick fighting.

It was brilliant fun and we all got quite good considering we were only at it for one day. It was hard work though and we worked solid all day in the sun. I think we knew we were getting better when we didn't have our concentration faces on and we could fight and give some sort of angry expression too.

After a long day and a long drive home due to lots of flooding I got a call from the agency.

"Hi John, Sorry but you will no longer be required for Merlin next week due to cost cutting so they're cutting down on the extras.

I never actually found out if this was true as one the the agencies favourite extras said to me that he wasn't cancelled. It was another TV show I stopped watching. I tried to call the other agencies to get work for next week but it was too late.

Wednesday 7th September 2008 – Lewis – SOCO

This was a lunchtime call near Oxford and the crew were off filming when I arrived so I had to sit and wait most of the afternoon. I was told to wear a suit but when costume saw us, we were told to wear a big white condom outfit over the top of the suit.

I didn't really know what a SOCO was and this was my first time playing one (Scene of Crime Officer) and I felt very silly. (Now I play one most weeks on Midsomer Murders and have done on many shows so don't think anything of it – remember you have to loose any self respect being an extra)

We got into costume but had to wait until the final scene of the day. It was funny how much effort the costume department spent on our ties under the outfit as we were on a wide shot, in the dark in a maze. I met an extra called Paul who was really nice and down to earth. I think Paul and I had more fun taking photos of each other in the outfits than anything as we really didn't do much this day.

It was just a wide shot of the maze that the body (Or lack of as it was so far away) was dumped in.

We had to wait until it got dark so it was a long afternoon just sitting around and eating (as extras do) and finally when it got dark enough we got called to set and we just bent over the fake body and that was it. Shot done and we could go home!

September

I got a call saying that Tony Jopia and Steve Bishop would like to have a chat with me about a role.

We went out to dinner and they told me that they had set up their own company in Wednesbury, in the West Midlands and had been given finance from Screen West Midlands amongst others to put together a Kids show TV pilot. Would I like to play the monster in it?

I pointed out that I was out of work and would like to help. I bagged the Production Manager Job but to be fair, they were only paying a couple of crew and I wasn't one of them but I still had redundancy money in the bank and if this pilot sold, I would be offered a role within the crew as a runner or something.

I spent the next few months putting the sets together and getting props.

Someone hit the back of my Rover and wrote it off. This wasn't good as I only got half the money I'd paid for not that long ago and so I went even further downhill with a 1999 Ford Mondeo (and to think I was waiting for a new car just a few months back)

Friday 12th September 2008 – Doctors – Nicholas

I got called to do Doctors on an afternoon shoot but meeting on location at a Golf club.

I was there early but I guess the agent knew I would be there already as she called and asked me to let the other extras know when they arrived that the crew was an hour behind and when they do turn up, we're not to go inside but wait out in the car park.

I wish it wasn't me as I know that pisses extras off when another extra has to pass information on.

My friend Paul (from Lewis) was booked to play a Character called Nicholas and had a line or two on the episode but when we were finally brought onto set, the 1st AD decided that I was to play Nicholas instead.

The role was nothing much, an actress says "Hello Nicholas, where's Joanna?" and I let her know she's over there somewhere talking to someone and pointed out some girl who ended up being my wife all day. I pointed this story out simply because Joanna became my real life partner many months later.

Monday 15th September 2008 –

Shameless – Posh School Dad

I got a call from the agency to say I was back on Shameless and there were 2 of us. One of us would have a speaking role while the other would not. Extras never excited by this sort of thing as it's usually always the other person who gets it.

I went to set and met the other extra and we were sent to meet the director. It was Paul Walker again and he just said "Hello John" in a kind of "You've already been featured so I don't really want you on set" kind of a way.

The trouble now was that I was doing this for the money and not to have fun with bigger roles. Bigger roles usually mean you can't come back on a show but if you're just in the background then no one seems to notice you.

Of course the other chap got it!

Tuesday 16th September 2008 –

Mitchell and Webb show – Reporter

One of the things I really love about having given up smoking is the fact I no longer have people begging for cigarettes all day on set.

We had to be back in London at 06.00 in the morning for this shoot and I had just got back from Manchester and yet I had managed to buy cigarettes at a garage and had never run out on set because I buy them.

There's this one chap in particular that every time I see, no matter what time of day , he never has any cigarettes. It must annoy me as I still remember him coming onto this shoot.

As soon as I saw him I knew what he was going to ask. "Morning Ian" I said

"Hello mate" he replies, he has no recollection (To this day) of my name but always remembers that I smoke. This was about the third time I had worked with him and had already got to know what he's like. "You haven't got a spare cigarette that you'd like to give me would you?"......grrrr

Anyhow, on this day they had about 6 sketches which were to be used one per episode. It was about a superhero with amazing powers but with the manners of a pig.

They would shoot toward to the actors and then turn around and shoot the extras.

The next scene would start on the extras and then move toward the actors. This was done to save on the amount of times they need to set the cameras up.

I did very well all day keeping a straight face and it's even easier when you've seen a rehearsal several times but there was this one sketch that was so funny and unfortunately it was one of the takes when they started on the extras so I didn't have time to hear it so often that it was no longer funny.

It was so tough keeping a straight face and I just had to think of bad things happening and the like so that I wouldn't crack up.

I saw the Behind the scenes chaps working and asked who they got the work through. "Oh, I'm one of the writers" he says. It's at this point I started to realise that behind the scenes was a "Who you know" job.

11th October 2008 –

Sherlock Holmes – Upper-class Gentleman

This was such a long day for what we got used for.

There were about 50 of us booked for today and we had to go to base to get ready and then we were picked up to go elsewhere for lunch and then we were taken to location base which was around the corner from St Paul's Cathedral.

The scene was just extras walking past Edward Fox's screen house in the day and then again when it got dark.

It was weird on set because the tourists in London came by in there hundreds to watch the filming. They kept taking photos non stop between takes. I'd never seen anything like this on a set before.

We did the walk past several times. I finally got to see Robert Downey Jnr. as Sherlock Holmes but it was no secret what he looked like as there were hundreds of paps there as well.

After the first scene was complete I had a quick peep into the tent where Guy Richie was sitting watching it all on the monitors. I just thought I'd have a look at the monitors and then I heard this voice "Come on in and have a look"

I turned and it was only Guy Richie talking to me. I wanted to say "You do realise I'm just an extra" but I figured he knew this already so I watched the rushes a couple of times and then went back outside.

Back outside I looked for the other extras and they were all having a group photo with Robert Downey Jnr. and then Joel Silver joined in for some photos. I ran up the steps to get in but it was too late, all the good ones had been taken. (I dint really mind as I was still so over the moon with Guy Richie letting me into the production tent)

Back in the base a bunch of sandwiches were delivered for the extras we had to be quiet as Guy Richie, Joel Silver, Robert Downey Jnr. and the stunt co-ordinator were talking through a big fight scene.

I sat by the sandwiches alone to read my book and stuff my face and then without warning after I had just stuffed a sandwich whole into my mouth, Robert and Joel walked back past me and said hello. What was I to do? I said hi back but with a mouthful of sandwich!

Spooked TV Pilot – Production Designer/ Teacher

This was the production I was asked to work on. I had never done anything like this before as I'm from a corporate background and sets were usually retail based but I spent months designing, buying begging and borrowing props and equipment for the sets of this low budget Kids show.

I was living off the redundancy and turned down a lot of work because this was more in line with the direction I wanted to go.

I learnt a lot on this production. Some good and some bad but it was so different being a part of the crew.

On one of the days we had a road to be set up to replicate World War 2 in the afternoon after setting up a French room at a school to be a Math's room in the morning.

We had finished the set up and were ready to go and put this road together.

The crew were in place, the 30 extras were sitting in place, the 2 main actors were on set and they were ready to go but the actor playing the teacher hadn't turned up.

They called the casting director but she was away and couldn't be reached so they needed a teacher and they needed one now!

I am not an actor! They wet my hair to make me look really slimy and gave me my lines. It actually went okay.

The show was never sold after it was finished but it gave me a greater understanding of how a shoot works.

Wednesday 12th November 2008 –

Torchwood -Children of the Earth– Mission Control

I thought I wasn't going to make it on this season of Torchwood as I had been cancelled from a couple of pencils but it was near the end of the shooting for the series.

I got a call to go down to the studio and I was going to be an extra for my first time on the show as I had always done doubling before.

I went to the studio and they had a costume ready for me. It turned out that we were going to do all five episodes in one day and we were a team at mission control who keep an eye on Captain Jack and his team's whereabouts.

It was a tiny set and there were 5 of us extras.

Being a geek I tend to wear a World War 2 style coat that has made it into so many period dramas but I had made the mistake of wearing it today without thinking.

I was sitting on the extras bus when I heard over the radio "Can I have John on set please". The runner said back into the radio "Which one is John?"

"The one in the Captain Jack coat!"

I was so embarrassed. I took it off and at the first opportunity threw it into my car.

The set was tiny and we were supposed to be some sort of phone operatives who keep an eye on Torchwood. All we really did was rotate chairs for each episode and pass about random photographs of tractors.

We had no idea why there were random photographs of tractors in the studio but we found them very amusing.

There was one scene in particular that had all the alarms going off and we were supposed to be in a state of panic but we had trouble keeping a straight face throughout the scene as every time we're told the alarm is going off my friend kept passing me this tractor photograph and telling me it's my new car (It seemed funny on the day) and we had such trouble keeping straight faces!

We had radio phones on our heads so during most of the takes what we're actually doing is pretending to be sales agents for every product we could possibly think of that amused us at the time.

All the scenes in the office for the whole 5 episodes were filmed in one day.

Friday 28th/Saturday 29th November 2008 –

Virgin Advert - Passenger

This, an advert to celebrate 25 years of virgin airways, was set in the 1980's in an airport. The airport in question was really Ascot race course but the production had done an amazing job of turning it into a 1980's airport.

There were about 200 extras on this and we were all given costume and props.

The advert was just a glamour looking aircrew walking through the airport and everybody having a gawp!

They had old video games that really worked as well as an "Our price" music store. The only down side was that is was jolly freezing and there was some serious waiting around but no where to sit.

I think every southern extra I knew was on the job.

For the most part I just went up and down the elevators for hours. We'd pass the same extras on the way up (Or down) and try to have something original to say or do each time. This got more and more difficult as the day went on .

Sunday 30th November/Monday 1st December 2008 –

Sherlock Holmes – Religious Zealot

Chattem Dock yard, in Kent. I was looking forward to this location as it's where my Pappa came from and used to work when he was young. He told me I should visit his sister and stay at her house. I did visit but decided not stay.

As I drove though the dock yard, I could tell why this was being used as a film location. They've kept a big part of it as it was and can easily double for London Docks.

I was also looking forward to working in this outfit as it looked like a fifteenth century Witch hunter costume.

They gave me a seriously unconvincing wig but it was cool to have long hair!

We had to wait most of the morning to finally be called on set on the first day. The scene was outside a prison and we wanted some chap to be released so lots of shouting involved and then Sherlock and Watson turn up in a stage coach. That was pretty much it and we did this for 2 days.

The weird thing was that if you turned around from the "prison gates" you'd see the main road going into town.

3rd December 2008 – Doctors – Dancing Bunny

I've said it before and I'll say it again. To be an extra you have to leave any self respect and dignity at home and just go with the flow and enjoy yourself.

This was a really, really cold day and I have no idea why my agent thought of me for this role but both myself and my friend Paul (Who's role I had stolen on this show when I played Nicholas) were booked as Dancing bunnies.

One of the characters in the show was leaving and the other Doctors were giving her a Chinese party as a send off. Even the director had no idea why 2 dancing bunnies had been booked for a Chinese party!

We started the scene with our heads on and stood on either side of the stage as some of the actors mimed songs they'd recorded earlier.

The great thing with giant heads is that you can twist the head as if it's facing camera and turn your real head to see the other Rabbit. This meant our dancing was very much in time. Our dancing was rubbish but always looked cool as the costumes were brilliant.

After this first scene we went outside into the frost to cool down. It was flipping hot inside the outfits and dancing inside a giant outfit is bound to make you sweat!

Extra Time

In the next scene it was lots of slow dancing and the brilliant 3rd AD gave us free reign to do as we pleased. So we took our giant Bunny heads off and danced together. It was the campiest thing I'd ever done on TV and I think perhaps the campiest thing to appear on Doctors yet!

We pretty much spent the whole day just dancing in the giant outfits and what started out as a really embarrassing job, we embraced and really enjoyed it.

We heard that we had been needed again but they forgot to book us so someone else came in to double for one of us and never got to take his head off so the audience wouldn't know it wasn't one of us.

Chapter Three

2009

Tuesday 6th January 2009 – Holby City – Anesthetist

I got a call to do Holby City. It was my first time on the show and working in BBC Elstree. A usual I got there early and parked up outside the gates for an hour or so until I had the courage to enter the gates. It's the first time I was nervous for a job since Doctors.

I don't know why I always get scared when I'm going to a TV studio. I think I just worry I'll not know where to go and end up looking stupid in front of other extras who all know where they're going.

I parked in the extras car park and security pointed me into the direction of the Holby studios.

It was easy to find considering the size of the complex and I got signed in by the AD and got given a costume and a script!. I was booked as an Anesthetist but I wasn't supposed to be a regular one from Holby City Hospital but a friend of one of the characters.

Today we were going to operate on a dog. I met the real dog whilst waiting to be taken to set.

On set I spotted John who usually worked on prosthetics on Doctor who and it turned out that his partner had worked for us on our TV pilot. It didn't cross my mind why John was even on set.

I went to set and saw the same dog that I'd met in the corridor on my way here. He was lying on his side and staying very still indeed.

It took a good ten minutes or so to realise that the dog was a fake and that's why John was here to operate and look after it!

The on set medical advisor showed me the basics of the Anesthetic Machine and all I had to do all day was play with the buttons and pretend I knew what I was doing.

In the scene I get introduced as a friend of Paul Bradley and a jazz musician and have to give a nice knowing smile for my very own close up. I know it sounds sad being excited by a close-up but Extras don't tend to get them very often so it's nice when we do.

I got to meet Rosie Marcel and Amanda Mealing and they were all so nice and down to Earth.

It was freezing in the studio and we were supposed to be in a basement doing a secret operation on the dog but Rosie saw I was cold and she asked costume to get me some heat-pads. It was nearly 2 years later before I saw her again to say thank you.

Because I was featured as a guest Anesthetist I figured I wouldn't be allowed back on the show again as the same character.

At lunch time I went to the canteen and it turned out that both Eastenders and Holby city not only share the same studio but also the same canteen. There was June Brown and Barbara Windsor having lunch on the next table. *Brilliant*!

Tuesday 13th January 2009 –

Ashes to Ashes – Dawid Czarnecki

I had finally got Ashes to Ashes. I was dying to do this show as I loved Life on Mars so much. I was booked as a Polish worker called Dawid Czarnecki

To do Ashes and have a named character was brilliant.

The plan was that I do a scene at a later date alive but today I was being booked as dead and covered in cement as they had dug me out a cement pit!

I got to set and signed in. Then I was taken to costume. I hate it when I'm not forewarned but it came as a shock when they gave me one small pair of flesh coloured pants as my entire costume.

He also gave me a dressing gown for when I was changed.

Then I was sent to make-up typically they were all girls. Not a bad thing when they're putting your face on but I had to lose the gown and stand there in my Flesh coloured pants whilst they both painted my body top to bottom with cement looking stuff plus I had to have chain marks on my ankle and Polish writing on my arm.

Whilst standing there looking naked and dirty with two ladies at my feet, the door suddenly opens and in walks Keeley Hawes.

She didn't even act surprised by the naked looking figure in front of her, she simply held out a hand and introduced herself.

The set was another walk down the road from the base but most people were on set by the time I was called so I had to walk up the road on my own to the set. I was bare footed and walking up the road looking like I'd just got out of bed with my dressing gown on but with a grey head and face!

At the set door, I was met by the runner and a chap named Charlie Roe who played the pathologist. He was shown to his dressing room whilst I was taken to the kitchen to wait. It was nice to finally meet the other extras who work as DCI's on the show. I have since become very good friend with Jack and Adrian

I had to wait a while and then before I was taken to set, I was taken into another make-up room for touch-ups. The other main actors were there and they were very nice to me.

Then I was taken onto set and put onto the slab. The slab is simply a very cold metal bed that you lie on when you die. I had a blanket for some of my back as it was very cold but wouldn't take long to warm up again.

I lay there with a towel over my flesh coloured pants and then a cloth placed over my entire body.

The Pathologist lent over to talk to me, he smiled and said "How come you get a name and I'm just Pathologist and I've got fucking lines!"

I replied "That's why you have a dressing room and I get shoved into the kitchen!"

The first AD introduced himself and introduced Keeley Hawes and Philip Glenister. I said Keeley and I had already met but then I tried to say something nice to Philip. I wasn't watching the "Demons" show that he had done and that was currently on TV but I'd heard it had had a slating so I said "Hello Philip, I'm really enjoying "Demons" right now.

Instead of the expected "Thank you" Philip looked at me and said "Well you're the only fucking one"

I figured I'd not mention it again and realised I'd not learnt that lesson ages ago like I thought I had. Do not mention other shows to actors!"

They talk about my body and the marks and writing on my arm for the scene. I had to take a breath in the middle of it as it was nearly 2 minutes long. Holding your breath on TV is far tougher than in real life as there is a sort of pressure you're under not to mess it up.

It was a fun scene and once again I was nearly naked on one of my favourite shows (Dr who, Torchwood, Sarah Jane and now Ashes to Ashes)

With the scene complete the crew and actors said goodbye but I had to wait as Art Department wanted photos to be used later in the episode. I found it weird watching the episode with the characters handing out my photos to people asking if they knew who I was.

Art Department finished and I was cleared to go.

I asked if I could look around the studio as I was a fan of the show and they were happy for me to have a wonder. I wish I was clean enough to have had my photo in the Police station. It was bigger in real life than I had expected.

I had to walk back to base on my own again and I spoke to the 2nd AD about getting cleaned up prior to going home.

He found me a spare room with a shower and it was nice to finally get that stuff off me. I'd left marks everywhere I had been and I'd not been able to go to the toilet!

I was booked to come back on the Friday but figured this is where I actually die.

Friday 16h January 2009 –

Ashes to Ashes - Dawid Czarnecki

It hadn't been long since I had done this show and I was really looking forward to coming back as I figured this was the day I die. I had a late call time but got there early.

I went to base and signed in and was told to wait. I decided to look at the really nice Bentley that was parked at the base. I guessed it was for the actors.

I was asked to go to costume but they only had a shirt and jumper for me. Not anything for waist down. I asked why and it turned out that I was only having my photograph taken for a passport that was being used in the show.

Disappointed but I guessed that meant I would get another day on the show. I went to make-up and then waited to go to set.

The 2nd AD told me to get into the car. "The Bentley?"

"Yes, It'll take you to set" he said

I didn't understand why I was being driven to set this time when I look perfectly normal but when I was covered in cement there I had to walk!

I got in the car. Wow. It had leather seats and everything but it was over all too quick as set is literally up the road.

I went inside to be greeted by the runner and then sent up to the art department. She asked me to stand by the wall for a few photos and that was it. I was done!

It had to be the quickest time on set ever. The car took me back to base where I changed and went to see the 2nd AD to sign out. I asked if I was due back for the death scene but it seems that scene was cut.

Monday 19th January 2009 –

Home time – The Prof (Burger man)

This was a comedy show for Channel 4 – I think. It was filmed in Coventry which is quite unusual. I was sitting on the bus and was asked to go outside to meet the director and the writer. I was baffled by this but did as I was told.

It turned out my receding hairline got me a walk-on on this show. There's a Burger man called "The Prof" in the show and he's supposed to be based on the writer.

I got to speak to the writer about the role but still didn't really understand why a burger man in a burger van was supposed to his alter ego.

They asked me to shout in my best Coventry accent "Burgers, get your burgers here"

Unfortunately I'm from down south and it sounded more London than Coventry so I guessed I would be dubbed over.

The burger van looked really hot as it was very bright inside and lots of steam came out when I opened the front. The other extras walking past made lots of comments on how lucky I am being in the warm but it was freezing plus I had to short sleeved!

I never saw the show so I have no idea even if burger man made it into it.

Wednesday 21st January 2009 –

Law and Order UK – Solicitor

This was a brand new show and I had heard both Freema Agyman (From Doctor who) and Jamie Bamber (From Battlestar Galactica)were on it. I was looking forward to it.

I wasn't in a scene with Freema but we bumped into each other and she said Hi and we briefly talked about her small role in Survivors.

The scene was Jamie Bamber, Bradley Walsh, another actor and myself in the interview room and all I had to do was take notes for the other actor as if I was his solicitor but I got a call during the day from my friend to ask if I had seen last nights episode of Battlestar Galactica? I said I hadn't and would have to wait for the DVD release.

He told me that they had given away who the final Cylon was. This was a bad thing as I knew everyone would be talking about it and I would find out before I actually got to see it.

I sat down with the actors and I told Jamie what had happened and as I would soon find out the final Cylon without wanting to, would he mind being the one to ruin it for me as it would be pretty cool that if it's going to get ruined, why not from the main actor of the show.

He told me not to worry and last nights episode was a red herring so sit tight and don't read anything until I get to watch the show.

Wednesday 28th January 2009 –

Sherlock (TV Pilot) – Policeman

I got a call asking if I was available to do Sherlock in Cardiff. I figured it must be the Guy Richie film and it had now moved to Cardiff.

I agreed to the job prior to finding out that it was a night shoot. This was an issue as I had to be on the other side of London by 07.00 the next morning for another show.

I thought nothing more of the job but was a little baffled when I turned up and we were sharing a base with Doctor who. I thought it rather a small base for a Hollywood movie.

It was only when I went to costume and got given my outfit that I realised it wasn't the Guy Ritchie movie at all but was a modern day TV show.

It was a TV pilot and tonight's scene was the very end of the episode. It was a single shot of a five minute scene so it took hours to choreograph the whole thing.

Before we got to set with our Police outfits on we were spoken to by the AD. They told us it was an offence to pretend to be police on the streets and we had to cover our outfits at all times. We already knew this but I've mentioned it here for a reason.

We got taken to set and rehearsed the scene over and over. I wasn't to join the scene until half way through.

As we were filming on the streets of Cardiff, real life passer bys were prone to walk past and at one point we had 4 chaps who had come out of the pub who were being a little naughty and refusing to get out of the way.

The scene had started and they were rolling cameras whilst I stood back as I don't enter the scene yet but my coat was off and I was in full Police uniform.

One of the crew members went up to the guys and asked if they wouldn't mind moving as they were prone to being in shot at any moment. They refused to get out of the way so someone else asked me if I would go and ask them to move. This is the same crew that made such a big deal out of pretending to be a police officer earlier and here they were getting me to ask these chaps to move. I knew why they asked me so I went up to them and politely asked them just to move around the corner a little.

They were a little hesitant at first as they weren't sure if I was a real policeman but as they were filming the show and I wasn't in shot they must have figured I was and moved.

I was starting to panic on this show because I was worried about getting to set in the morning.

Lunch time I swapped base to say hi to the Doctor who crew. They were filming "Planet of the Dead" just down the road and the scene was that a bus had gone into a tunnel but never comes out. I really wanted to swap shows and I was already in the right uniform but unfortunately it doesn't work like that.

I thought that as we only had one scene that we would be wrapped quite early but it was a tough scene and so many things kept going wrong.

We finally wrapped at 03.45. The other extras knew I was desperate to go so they let me get changed first. I ran to the changing room, changed, threw my uniform back to costume, ran to the production office and jumped into the car.

I had set Sat Nav up earlier and so I turned it on and went as fast as I could. I didn't it make a mile down the road when I saw that the tunnel had been blocked for filming! In real life I would have stopped and watched the filming as it was Doctor who but in this case I had no love for the show what so ever and took the long way round to get out of Cardiff. It was 178 miles to the next location. I drove as fast as I could and made it out set at 06.50. Just in time for a coffee and to sign in!

Thursday 29th January 2009 –

Desperate Romantics – Art Collector

I was so tired this day that I don't really remember much. It was some BBC drama and we were supposed to be posh art collectors but it was back when the BBC still had costumes and they were the oldest costumes ever with rips all through them.

There was a male extra who was going nude for a scene and it was his fist time going nude on TV. I had a lot of respect for him. I couldn't do it!

He was really scared and wasn't helped by the fact that the runner came onto the bus making fun of the fact that it's really cold and he'll shrink in the weather!

After years of being an extra I found a new problem on this day. There were 2 of us standing next to each other pretending to look at a painting and the camera was set up to face us. We had to talk (Mime) about how good this painting was but of course we were standing next to each other and couldn't see each others mouths. We couldn't even whisper as the actors were right next to us giving dialogue.

We ended up taping each other with our elbows to when it was time for the other to talk otherwise it would have looked like we were both talking at the same time. (Do look out for extras that do this on a regular basis on TV)

I was so tired and this proving to be a really long day. I had been up since yesterday morning and I was now booked for Eastenders the following day. At least Eastenders was only down the road from my London residence. I then got the call I'd been waiting for for months! "Hi John, Are you available to double for an actor on Doctor who?"

"Yes, when" I replied with a smile!

"Tonight"

AAAAAAAAAAAAGH! How could this be? Can I turn this job down? Can I drive another 178 miles back to Cardiff on the hope of making it in time and get back to Willesden Court house by 08.00 the next morning?

I had to say no! I can't believe I had to turn Doctor who down just because of sleep but there was no way I could have done it. Typical

Friday 30th January 2009 – Eastenders – Solicitor

Not a special day by no means but it was my first time on Eastenders. I would have liked to have been in the studio but this was a nice easy day. I got checked by costume and make-up and was sent into the courtroom to wait for the scene. I expected a courtroom scene but it didn't happen. I sat and waited most of the day and ended up falling to sleep.

A few hours later we got called to set and it wasn't a court scene after all, we just had to walk through the foyer whilst a couple of actors spoke before going to court. Brilliant. Nice and easy.

Saturday 31st January / Sunday 1st February 2009 –

No Justice, Just Us - Spider-man

I was introduced to a producer called Dominic Took who wanted to put a short film together and so he hired the Spooked TV pilot team, writer Stephen Bishop and one of the co-directors, Tony Jopia.

Stephen had written a short story based on the fathers for justice who had kidnapped a minister's son but he had died in transit.

I helped put the crew together and Tony gave me a small part with a couple of lines. I'm not an actor and have never claimed to be one but I was cool with this tiny part dressed as a super hero. The night before filming, Dominic called me and said that one of the actors had dropped out and would I mind getting some more dialogue? I said "No thank you" and I knew I was incapable of acting (Giving an extra lines does not make him an actor!)

He believed in me and said it would help the production out tremendously at this late stage of pre -production so I finally agreed and appreciated his confidence.

I spent the night trying my hardest to learn all the new dialogue I'd been sent.

The next day I went to set and the real actors helped me out an awful lot and told me what was good and what was bad and how to change h way I was saying things.

By the Sunday I really felt the character I was playing. It was weird because it made everything easier once I understood the person I was playing.

I enjoyed the second day far more both because I knew my lines plus I understood what the character wanted. (Whether I was any good is another question) but it was great working on a production again. I'm much happier having some sort of creative control of a production than I am in front of the camera. Although I enjoy them both.

Thursday 26th February 2009 –

Spooked TV Pilot re shoots – Production Design

The pilot of Spooked that Tony and Graeme had directed had been edited and even had a small première in a theatre in Birmingham.

CITV had been approached and liked the 45 minute pilot but had requested a much shorter pilot episode so a re edit had to be done and a few re-shoots to simplify the show.

We had a lot of shots to get in, in just one day but we managed it and everybody pulled out all the stops to make sure we completed on time.

Later in April after all the changes had been made in accordance to CITV's requests, we were turned down to have it made into a series.

It was an experience though and I learnt so much about working with a bigger crew than I was used to.

Monday 2nd March – Cast off – Passing businessman

It's not often we get to film in Nottingham but I was told in advance that this was a very low budget TV show so extras were a luxury to them!

My agent was so nice she even offered to pay for my parking as free parking in Nottingham town centre in pretty impossible.

I turned up in the road I was booked for early. I knew it was low budget but really did expect to see at some sort of life there. It was empty, not even a security man or any bollards on the road. I sat in the car and waited until my call time (07.00) but still nothing. It was too early to call the agency but I figured they would call me if there was a problem.

I waited about an hour and then text the agency just in case. I didn't really want to wake them up but I was equally baffled why no one had called me to find out where I am!

I parked up and stood in the filing street.

A text came through so I checked it and it was from my agent. She was equally baffled and gave me the main base number. I called but no one answered. I left a message to mention I'm at location and am waiting, am happy to wait as long as everyone knows I'm not late.

Another hour passed and it crossed my mind to go home but my agent was also trying to get in touch with the production.

Then out of the blue, an old car turns up and drops off a young lady with bags of clothes and an ironing board!

I went to say hello as I had guessed this was a member of the costume department. It sure was and she had got this lift but was wondering where the rest of the crew was!

She phoned her work mate and they said they'd been held up but would be along soon and could I hold all the costume in my car until they arrived! (I'd never been asked that before)

The thing with this show that made me want to mention it was that it was one of those productions where everybody does it for love far more than for money. All the crew were doubling up and working their socks off to make a brilliant show and they were all so down to earth. I was introduced to the director and the first AD and asked to have breakfast and lunch with them and it was although I was an equal. It was so nice and not something we see on set very much.

The actor playing the blind chap really was blind and had his script in brail. I'd not seen that before either and hadn't even thought about how blind actors read scripts (I'm sure they usually get sighted actors to play blind people)

My role really was just to walk down the street and glance at the blind guy and then walk off. Nothing more. I'd love to have worked with that crew.

Friday 6th March 2009 –

Partners in Care photo shoot - Patient

I must surely have a specific look as I was booked to play a mentally ill patient for a booklet to advertise the facilities of a care home.

This was a truly fun day out as I had to go to the home and meet the customers of the booklet and the people putting the booklet together.

They talked me through the booklet photos and what they were looking for.

There were 2 patients and 2 carers for the shoot and we went all around the village (Near Gloucestershire) for shoots.

My first time ever at a gym in my life. Is that bad? I just had to use the equipment and have a little blank look on my face (Nothing new there)

We also went to the garden centre and I went in to character obviously too well as the lady in the Garden centre really thought I was a patient. I didn't let on either way and she showed me how to move the flower pots from the basket onto table and then even showed me how to water the plants.

We went back to the home for lunch and then one more trip out to the corner shop to do some shopping. That was also fun as I had a carrier basket and just went into character around the shop putting things into the basket (I don't think the shop keeper was amused when I filled the basket with pineapples and tampons)

I wish they'd call me back to do some more shoots.

They also very kindly sent me a PDF of the leaflets and I had made it to the cover of one of them!

Sunday 15th March 2009 -

Foyles war – Russian House Servant/ British Soldier

I was booked as a Russian House servant and as a British Soldier on this show. I was playing the Russian in the morning and it was just me so it was one of those nice mornings where you're treated so much as an extra but more like a person.

I had a nice short back and sides haircut. This job is Okay if you don't want to ever pay for a haircut again plus they pay you to cut your hair.

My scene was jolly easy as all I had to do was see some guy up the stairs.

He was a really funny actor who was such a bad influence. I got on really well with him but he wanted to run down the stairs backward between takes and even suggested we do it on a take. Something some people fail to understand if they've not spent a long time on set is that actors can do about anything they want to on set. "Can everyone be quiet on set please" does not seem to apply to actors and if they're naughty then it's funny.

This is not the same for an extra. If you're naughty, you're shouted at, put back into place and your agent is told so it will affect future work.

Hence why I was unable to play running up and down the stairs backward. That's pretty much my morning story as a Russian. I was the sent over to change as fast as I could to play a British Solider.

That reminds me too. Extras can sit around all day with nothing to do but wait until we're called for but when you are suddenly asked to change, it's as if you should have done it five minutes before they asked you to. You'll never be able to do it quick enough.

So I changed into a British uniform and met the other 2 extras who were going to do the next scene with me.

The scene was that I am now about to arrest the chap that I just took upstairs when I was Russian.

Steve, the 3rd AD asked that I stay at the back of the other 2 soldiers as I was so well seen this morning.

The director had other ideas. He liked my accent and this was a small speaking role as I had to say something like "You're under arrest, you're coming with us"

So, I ended up being at the front of the soldiers. Who needs continuity? We had to march him down the stairs and to the door but the external of the door was at another location that we were going back to soon.

Wed 25th March 2009 – The Bill – Policeman

On a show like "The Bill" they have regular policemen and CID in the show but in between the gaps of the scenes they have something called establishing shots.

These tell the audience where the next is taking place (in accordance of the show and not necessarily in real life)

So that the establishing shots can be slotted into the show at any time in any episode they deliberately don't use any police-men or CID that are in the show so that there are no continuity issues.

This was an establishing shot day so we spent the whole day outside the police station walking about, backwards and forwards and into cars and back out. It went on for 12 hours and was a tad tiring.

The Police station in the Bill used to be an external set that was in the middle of a trading estate but all the signs for the station were taken down between shoots.

They had all the signage up and all the lights on at the station and whilst we were doing one take, a car pulled up and a girl got out thinking it was a real police station.

The security explained that this was just a set and they later told me it happens all the time when they set up the station.

We did loads and loads of episodes worth on this day.

Thursday 26th March 2009 – Spooks – Russian agent

I'm showing my ignorance by saying this but I don't watch much TV and I thought Spooks was about ghosts and not spies and things.

I was playing a Russian in this episode and myself and the other Russians walk into a room and face the British. I think that's all we did.

My mind was on other things as I had a call from the agency to ask if I would be willing to shave my head to be in Doctor who next week for 4 days and that I would be painted white! I was over the moon. They're filing the Christmas and New year David Tennant Doctor who send off and I was going to be in it. I wouldn't offer to have a head shave for much else but this is Who. This is what started me doing the Extra work.

I asked if it was absolutely booked and it was so I turned down any other work I was being offered for it.

The rest of the day I was on such a high on set and still can't remember if we did anything else of interest on spooks.

The next evening I got a call to let me know that Doctor who was changing dates and I'm being re-scheduled.

I'm still waiting for that re-schedule!

Sunday 29th March 2009 –

Day of the Triffids – Blinded Bearskin Soldier

I'm not one for asking to do particular work (well except for Dr who and that's why I guess they no longer want me do the show) but I love John Wyndham books and hadn't been asked to do Triffids so I called the office and explained how much I love the show and that I really would very much like to be on it.

The agent said that she only had 2 roles left to be filled and they were both costume. She checked my sizes and said I was to small to it the outfits. I was disappointed but completely understood. She then added that it wouldn't be a problem changing my sizes on the system and to make sure I was well padded on the day! Brilliant. I was booked as a Bearskin.

I got to base and was given a "Triffids Film Unit Vehicle" permit for the car. That was one brilliant way to start the day. I instantly took a photo of it!

There were loads of us but only a few in uniforms so I was called into costume early to get ready. It was so obvious that the uniform didn't fit.

I tried to pad it out with T-shirts but there were only 2 of us in that outfit and the other chaps fit perfectly well so it was rather obvious mine didn't.

There must have been at least 250 extras on set that day. The scene was that all the blind public are trying to get through the gates and we're on the other side of the gates with a few policemen and CID and shooting at the public; *Even though we are all blind.*

The location was near the back of Downing Street, just off Trafalgar square and due to this we would be unable to really fire blanks from our guns due to terrorist fears. Thanks terrorists, we lost the extra money because of your stupidity!

It take more "acting" skills to pretend to fire a gun as opposed to firing blanks as we have to fake the recoil from the weapon.

It was a fun scene and pretending to shoot at the crowd although I aimed upward as to not look particularly accurate.

The prop people threw tons of paper out of the windows (It looked pretty cool but one does wonder why people are throwing paper out of a window whilst being shot at)

They did an angle from the back of us and I was asked to walk in (a blind walk) so I decided to really close my eyes. I'm not sure if that was a good idea as I could have walked into something or fallen over.

When we were shooting at the crowd, the camera came right up to me so I gave it my best blind mad shooty pose! I refused to blink and my eyes were watering like mad. How could they not use such a scene? (They didn't)

To be fair, I didn't mind not being seen as I was just glad to spend a day on the Triffid set.

At lunch time the two Bearskins were wrapped as we could not be used to double up. We left the location but on the way back to base we struggled to get through the crowds of tourists as they must have thought we were real bearskins. We didn't have our hats on, our top buttons were undone and we had nasty greasy hair but that didn't deter people from thinking we were the real thing They kept stopping us for photos with them and then when we would try to go again, someone else would ask. Plus someone was videoing us and had their video camera in our faces all the way from set to base. It was quite a weird experience.

Thursday 9th April 2009 –

Foyles War – British Soldier/ 2 x Passer bys

The Hair and Make-up girl was new. I mean she was very new. I don't think she's ever cut hair before.

This was supposed to be continuity to the last time we did this and we 3 British soldiers were taking the Russian chap out to the car from the scenes we had already filmed indoors but suddenly we had really bad very short awful haircuts. She spent 45 minutes hacking away until there was not much left she could do to ruin it any more! What did I say earlier about getting paid for haircuts? Now I know why they pay us!

The haircut from hell!

We were filming out on the street. The guys had done a fantastic job of making the whole street look like it's 1940's.

We bring the actor down to a waiting vehicle and off we go out of this scene but the show goes on and the next scene is Mr Foyle himself walking out of the same building but being watched by a spy.

Rather than waste money and send us home, they decided that they could double us again and this time I became not one but 2 people in the street. I quickly got changed and then walk up the street in the scene and then when out of shot, I take off the jacket and walk back down the street.

Extra Time

There were a good few paparazzi around which was weird as I didn't think it was an exciting enough show for paps to take photos.

The spy was played by a new actor and this was his final day. There were also a whole bundle of fantastic classic cars on set.

The scene had the spy watching Mr Folye and reversing out the road. They did the scene several times but on the last time they wanted an angle from inside the car so the reversing mirror got moved so that the camera man in the back of the car could see the actors face and it looks like (from our point of view) that the actor can see out the mirror. He in fact could not.

They turned over, action. The car starts to reverse and you heard all the crew shout "Whoa" when all of a sudden there was a crash and silence. I mean the whole of London went into silence.

The car had reversed into the next classic car which in turn shoved into the next classic car and it brought with it the eeriest silence I have ever witnessed on set.

The 3rd AD was the first to wake up from this strange coma. He barked orders that they move the cars around the corner. Take photographic evidence of the accident and get on with the next shot.

The poor actor wanted the world to open and swallow him there and then.

I was actually walking past the car when it happened and I think even I stopped mid scene to gasp. We're told not to stop no matter what until we hear cut in case some material can be used.

Everybody was cool about the accident and it wasn't long until we were back working.

Tuesday 21st April 2009 – Spooks – Russian Agent

It was lucky I didn't get my head shaved for Doctor who as I was asked to come back as this Russian chap on Spooks. This was filmed down near Croydon and we were supposed to a group of Russian agents enjoying lap dancing at a club.

TV and film is weird sometimes because you may thing this was a fun day but when you do things like this for TV, it's just work and not remotely sexy. (Although now I've said that I did notice more continuity photos than usual being taken on set this day)

There were a small group of us sitting in the club whilst the girls danced and we were enjoying ourselves watching and I think one of the agents goes outside and gets murdered. I'm not there to find out and have yet to watch "Spooks"

Wed 22nd April 2009 – Holby City – Anesthetist

This was my first day as a semi-regular on Holby city. I get to play the same character over and over.

I was called back because they needed several male Anesthetists for a party. The actor who played one of us was leaving this day and we had to come out of the lift with bald hats on and bow ties.

On the first few takes we all come out doing the conga and singing but unfortunately the final version was a lot tamer and involved us all coming out of the lift and cheering that we're off to the pub! I think most of the crew preferred the first version.

Friday 24th April 2009 –

Four Lions (Skeleton Keys) – Passer-by

I got to the base in Leeds. This was a low budget film with pretty much every department based within two vehicles. The production office was in the back of our bus and so we were there when news of a potentially awkward incident reached the producer.

The police had spotted the second unit minibus behaving suspiciously and had stopped it. The film was a comedy about Muslim suicide bombers and the minibus was full of Asian actors with rucksacks. The police had taken the threat seriously and had had to call the production office to confirm that it was just a film! Brilliant

I've said before how much I enjoy working on Low budget films. I wish I had worked as crew on this production. Everyone was fantastic and down to Earth.

Our scene was just a tiny one near the end of the film with us walking away, but we were told that we would have to come back for continuity. Unfortunately I was double booked and couldn't make it.

Tuesday 28th April 2009 –

Married, Single, Other – Night clubber

I am surprised sometimes by what I get booked for and this was one of those days. Back in Leeds I was booked as a dancer in a club (along with around a hundred other extras).

The show starred Ralf Little and Dean Lennox Kelly with whom I got to have a great long chat at lunchtime and who remembered me from Doctor Who.

When we dance to music on TV, the music isn't there for us to hear. Usually no one even knows what song is going to be played.

All we get is a few beats to remember in our heads or if we are lucky and they know what the music is going to be, we get to hear a few seconds of the track.

So we had a whole dance floor of people dancing to nothing. This is done to get clean recordings of the dialogue. The actors also have to remember to speak up as there will be a music track put on so it sounds like they're speaking above the music.

I managed to get away with leaving the dance floor on action. To be fair I have no rhythm when there is music playing so there was no point in me being there!

Friday 1st May – Tuesday 16th June 2009 –
Gulliver's Travels – Lilliputian Soldier

This was the most time that I had ever spent on a single film. We started shooting at Blenheim Palace in Oxford shire and there were fifty Lilliputian soldiers to start with. We were asked to grow beards which were all cut into trendy shapes but I had decided not to grow one in case there were other shows that I had to go on.

We spent the first day learning to march. Some of the extras seemed to get a little confused and believe that they really were now in the army. I remember one ex-military extra coming up to us and saying "I've spoken to the crew and they say you've been paid to march so get it the fuck right or get off set." (I've told you that story for a reason).

We spent the first week pulling ropes, which we had to do so many times and from so many angles, as we were playing hundreds of people and so had to be replicated.

There were so many days on this and we were earning really nice money but we were working from six in the morning until nine at night so it got crazy. It wouldn't have been any nearer if I had stayed in London than it was staying in Birmingham, so the travelling was mad as well. We were working day after day, which at first it was great as we were thinking how much we were earning but then after a few days we just wanted a day off.

Two weeks into shooting, a message was sent around saying that the studio didn't like the beards so could we take them off. Luckily I'd not grown one in the first place. At least they didn't make us shoot the rope scenes all over again.

We did have to start doing shots both with and without hats just in case they changed their minds about that.

I got a whole host of new friends on this film including the regular extras from Ashes to Ashes with whom I get on very well.

On one of the days I was just lucky to be picked to be the soldier who brands Jack Black with a branding iron. It was weird because I was put on my own with the second unit team (the same one that does the Bond films), while the rest of the soldiers were wrapped.

I had to brand a mark on the green screen where Jack's leg would be.

I did this first of all with the green screen and a mark. The branding iron was very heavy and had to be wired through my sleeve to make it glow as if it were hot and steaming.

Someone had to hold the other end and give it a throw on action or I wouldn't have been able to lift it.

I then had to hold it still for two seconds to suggest that I was actually doing the branding, which was also hard work. It got tougher still when we did a 'clean plate' which is a version without the green screen and the little mark, so I had to get the position just right and hold it for two seconds.

I just couldn't get it right. By take eight the 1st AD told me semi-jokingly that I wasn't to worry or panic as everyone was now on overtime, and the entire production based in Blenheim Palace, which itself was costing £50,000 a day to hire, was just waiting for me to do the shot correctly. I was costing the whole production £1000 simply by not getting this shot right! So, no pressure then!

Many months later, I heard that they had replaced me with a big burly looking blacksmith type on the re-shoots.

The next location was Pinewood Studios. Here they had built a few massive sets and there were now another fifty extras dressed as soldiers.

Here we had the gates to the Palace and were supposed to be looking out to sea, although all we were really looking at was studio waste land. We were given marks on cranes to look at to get the correct eye level, as if we were looking at Gulliver.

Besides the hundred soldiers there were also a hundred and fifty or so villagers, so it took ages for us all to get ready every day. We were pretty much working fifteen hours a day.

Lunch time became an art form. Being a soldier meant that had to have weapons to hand in before eating, which the villagers didn't have. So I would pay careful attention to find out when lunch time was happening and then stand near the weapons tent.

They would call lunch and we would hand our weapons in and run to the extras food trailer. Only once did I get there first. What a feeling that was, running, way ahead of all the other 249 extras. That's what it must feel like to win an Olympic medal. I only wish I had taken my mobile telephone out to take a photo of this amazing feat. It was seriously the highlight of the day. I only got there first on the one occasion, but most the time I was in the first five. It was always the same few extras who ran like mad to get lunch.

If you weren't in the first fifty or so, it would mean a long wait and sometimes lunch could even finish before some people got it!

We would eat on the steps of the James Bond studio, which was something that I never got used to. This place was just one of those things that I had grown up wanting to see, and here I was, sitting on the steps. One day the doors were open at the side. I had to look inside. I'm not sure what I expected to see, maybe big Bond sets and the like, but it was just a big empty hanger with a dip in the middle, which looked like it could hold a submarine.

We spent most of our time marching, standing at attention and facing forwards. We always tried to avoid being among the ones who had to hold flags, although who was chosen for that was pretty much a lottery.

With such a late finish time and early call time, I sometimes wouldn't drive back into London and would stay over in a secret parking spot, sleep in the car and in the morning pop along to Beaconsfield service station to get cleaned up and shaved.

They were also filming scenes from the latest "Harry Potter" film and re shoots from "Wolf Man" at Pinewood, and we would often bump into the other extras and gossip about what scenes we were doing, although most of the time we would just be reacting in front of the green screen. The studio could probably have saved a fortune by using the same extras in the green screen room for all three films, just changing our clothes each time.

Our last day at Pinewood was a day of dance rehearsals. There must have been two hundred extras on set this day and we were broken down into small groups of ten, each with our own dance teacher.

We had to start with big warm ups. Nobody really knew what was going on and we all felt a little silly to start with. It turned out that there was a song in the film which we and Jack Black (Gulliver) all danced to. This was something that I had always wanted to do since I had watched "the Blues Brothers" when I was young, but it's not as easy as you might think.

Extra Time

I'm not a good dancer and even though we practised all day, I still struggled to get my head around all the moves.

The following day we moved location to the Royal Naval College at Greenwich, where so many films are shot. We were now going to spend a week doing a 3 minute dance routine.

I imagined that I would get a few days more practice to get it right and spent all morning in the extras tent practicing. I was delighted when we went on set as it looked as if I had been given a great place behind the actors where no one would see me.

WRONG

The camera was directly behind us and pointing right at me.

They started shooting, the music came on and we started to dance? We were awful. They had placed the real dancers up by the actors but it might have been a better idea to put them where we were.

They cut the cameras and the first AD came and shouted at us for not being in time. We had to do the whole dance in front of him there and then and anyone who got it wrong was sent to the back of the other section away from the camera.

At lunch time, one of the extras who seemed to think that he really was in the military was sounding off, complaining about how much he hated having to dance and about how we were being spoken to. It was the same guy who had earlier criticized our marching abilities. "Well," I told him, "I've spoken to the crew and they say that you have been paid to dance, so get it the fuck right or get off set". That was satisfying.

Five days in and I think I was just about starting to get it right. The scene took nearly a week to shoot and I'm told that it's still in the film.

The next week we changed location again moving to Aldershot Army Barracks.

The weather was amazing and it was just a super job. Here they had built lots of green screen walls and small parts of a city as I guess we were supposed to be in the town.

The uniform started getting more casual day by day. First we lost our hats, then the jackets went and our top buttons had to be undone. Some soldiers changed altogether and just wore casual T-shirts.

There were also noticeably fewer of us day by day. Gulliver was supposed to have changed our quaint little town into a mini-America, so and the older extras were being replaced by younger prettier ones as the town became trendy.

I kept expecting to be dispensed, with but somehow I survived. There we were, just a few of us oldies left as soldiers, surrounded by all these young good looking extras.

I had to keep turning jobs down on other shows because I was being so spoilt on this film. The money was brilliant but I didn't like to turn work down.

I didn't expect to go back onto Waterloo Road again because I'd turned it down so many times.

Sunday17th /Monday 18th May 2009 –

Breaking the Mould – Sales Agent

This was a BBC4 period TV movie about the discovery of Penicillin, which starred Dominic West and Denis Lawson. I was booked along with another chap as sales agents who wanted to buy the new discovery for business reasons.

I assumed all that Dominic and Denis would talk about would be Star Wars, which they were both in, but I never heard it mentioned once. In one a scene we we're sitting around a desk, applauding Denis Lawson for discovering Penicillin. In my head of course I was clapping for an entirely different reason. Denis had played Wedge in the Star Wars films, helping to destroy the Death Star in Return of the Jedi. I was clapping our rebel hero!

It was only a small production and everyone was really nice. It was the first time that I met Dominic West, who had just come from playing the lead in a major TV show in the States. I didn't expect him to as down to Earth as he soon showed himself to be.

The other extra turned out to be one of those people who pushed to the front at every opportunity. To be fair, we don't have many camera-hoggers in the extras community but this guy was so annoying. On every angle of every scene he would change position to make sure that he was at the front.

On the second day we weren't called in until after lunch, which usually indicates that we shouldn't assume that we are welcome to eat lunch.

I got there early and sat in the car while everyone ate but then I saw the other camera hogging extra so I got out the car and made a coffee.

The other extra came up to me with a plate full of food and asked if I was eating. I said I wasn't sure if we were allowed. Right on cue the 2nd AD came angrily up to us.

"You were both booked for after lunch for a reason. There are only so many people catered for and you've just taken other peoples food."

The thing was, he was talking to both of us. I had only had a coffee but I expect he just saw both of us as a pair. The other guy still got to eat his lunch but I didn't! I kind of wish I'd grabbed some food too as I had shared in the telling off.

This wasn't the first time this had happened to me. I had had a day on Waterloo Road not that long before with a 09.00 call time. I got there at 08.00 and went to breakfast. The catering woman questioned me about my call time

"I thought the teachers didn't start until nine!"

I replied that I had started early so as to get some breakfast.

"Someone will have to do without now," she said. "We only cook enough of the numbers we're given. I'll let you have a breakfast this time but don't come in early asking to be fed again!"

I had been told and had learnt my lesson.

Tuesday 23rd June 2009 - Poirot (Clocks) – Special Agent

Hayes, Middlesex. This was a blighter of a studio to find first time. Nonetheless I found it and it turned out to be a very friendly crew indeed. The 3rd came into the bus to see me and gave me the sides for the day. (Sides are the parts of the script that are being filmed on that particular day and are usually fixed onto the back of the call sheet). This doesn't happen very often but it's very nice when it does as we know then what the scene is about and how long we will be expected to be on set.

When I looked through the call sheet I saw Tom Burke's name. I froze. I knew that name. Tom was the one I loved in the film "I Want Candy" but when I had spoken to him he had hated it and wasn't afraid to tell me his thoughts on the film! I went to costume to get into my 1940s gear. I seem to spend a lot of time in period clothes..

It was a shame that David Suchet wasn't on set that day as I really wanted to see him working as Hercule Poirot.

My role was to walk some suspect or other to the cell... I think.

It was a set that had been made to look like some tunnels that they had filmed in down at Portsmouth. My friend Adrian was there who I had gotten to know on Gulliver's Travels. (He had been one of the regular CID guys on Ashes to Ashes).

On set I bumped into Tom Burke. I said hello and he returned the greeting. I knew he recognised me from somewhere and was terrified that he would realise that I was the one whom he had shouted at in Bristol.

He asked if we'd met before and I told him it was on another period piece in Bristol. "Oh In Love with Barbara" he said, although it hadn't been called that when we shot it

I said I thought it was called something else but he told me they'd changed the name of the show.

He had no idea that I was the "I Want Candy" fan.

Friday 26th June 2009 – Waterloo Road - Teacher

I had stopped enjoying Waterloo Road a while ago. A lot of the cast had gone onto other things and on this season they had merged Waterloo School with another school in order to explain the mass exodus of actors. (At least I imagine that was the reason, but don't quote me. Remember extras know nothing!).

Philip Martin Brown was still there and he's the best thing about the show. He plays such a bad guy on screen but is in fact the nicest down to earth guy there is.

This ended up being my last day on the show although I had done a few episodes that season. For every episode we had a different costume and we'd also have to take the costume we'd used with us. We were carrying around so much clothing that it was getting silly. To make things worse, they had stopped the extras from parking in the school car park so we had to walk further. I had always said when I stopped enjoying a job, I wouldn't do it again.

We were in the staff room, doing the usual walking about whilst the actors iterated. I was told to go into the kitchen, pour an orange juice then walk behind the actors, sit down and drink the juice.

We did a rehearsal and I pretended to get the orange juice and pretended to drink it from a pretend glass, which is the sort of thing we do on rehearsal, so as to save opening bottles and packets. It becomes perfectly normal to walk about with imaginary props. However, on this particular occasion, I had missed the clapper board – we were going for a take.

They did the scene and the director walked into the staff room from next door (where he had been watching on a monitor). He looked at me accusingly. "What was this man doing? Why was he pretending to drink from an invisible glass?"

I was so embarrassed. Maybe subconsciously that's why I never went back!

Tuesday 7th July – Friday 9th July 2009 –

Gavin and Stacey

This was one of those amazing jobs that you can't believe they pay you for. I'd never watched Gavin and Stacy so I wasn't really looking forward particularly to being on the show. I was more excited about being paid to sit at the seaside for three days in the sunshine.

My partner and I were both booked for this job in Barry Island. We booked a cheap hotel so we didn't have to travel.

The first two days were spent simply playing in the sand. It didn't matter when they said action or cut as we simply played in the sand all day.

The tide didn't come in until quite late and so they kept the reverses until then. The water was cold and although it still looked hot, there was a cold wind about.

The 3rd AD asked if anyone wouldn't mind getting into the water. I thought "why not?" and ended up regretting volunteering as the water was a lot colder than I had expected.

The next evening they asked for all the same people to go back into the water. I decided It was too cold and I didn't want to do it.

"But you must. It's continuity" I was told.

"Well, if you want me to go into the water, I want a walk-on" (which is another way of saying that I wanted more money).

They agreed, although in truth I wished they hadn't because I really didn't want to go back into the water).

On the third day we were off to film at the fair and they asked us if we'd mind going on the rides! Fancy being asked if you want to go on the rides at a fair and get paid for it. Brilliant! Plus they last a lot longer when they're filming them.

Friday 17th July - Survivors – Slave Miner

I was picked as a slave miner for Survivors. It was an automatic walk-on, which meant more money. I guess I only got it as I'm skinny.

The set on the first day was a massive empty estate in Worcestershire, which was to be the house of a man running a slave mining facility.

Make-up on this episode consisted of rags and a covering of black cream that was supposed to be coal dust. It wasn't very nice and we could hardly recognise ourselves.

Extra Time

We were doing our last scene first and this was seriously action packed. The stunt coordinator worked with each of us to make sure no accidents happened.

My first scene was running after, catching and hacking a guy up with an axe! It was my friend Sean. It's always nice when you get a juicy bit of action, especially if you get to kill a friend!

The timing had to be right and I catch up with him at the door. He's not able to go any further and I whack him in the back with the axe. He falls and I then take another swing into his face!

We were happy with this but alas, the word came down that the BBC wouldn't like so much violence, so we had to do it all again but this time using a spade! I'm not sure how hacking up a man with a spade is less violent than with an axe but who am I to argue?

In my next scene, I had to go a little mad and smash the tops off hundreds of wine bottles in the cellar, so that another slave miner could throw the bad guy into the broken necks of the bottles.

I gave it my all with the madness. We had been locked in a mine for months and now we were reaping our revenge!

I loved Survivors and I gave it my all, as this was one of the few shows on TV that I actually watched. After the day was over, I was really looking forward to doing it again.

Monday 27th July 2009 – Survivors – Slave Miner

It was ten days later when we were finally called back to Survivors which was now based in Moss Pit mining museum near Stoke-on-Trent.

It was great to see the same extras as last week but it wasn't long before we were sent to costume and then back into the make-up chair. Again, they had a pot of black cream that I was told to rub all over my hands as the make-up girl rubbed it into my face, my ears and my neck. My hair was then filled with soot.

The trouble with this sort of muck is that it takes forever to wash out of all the hard-to-get-at areas such as your ears only for it all to be put back in again the same the next day. However as we extras are never allowed the luxury of pride in our appearance from the moment we start work, it's nice at least to have a little bit when we turn up. It's nice to know that your hair and skin is all clean prior to them throwing everything back on you.

This set was a real life mine that had been turned into a museum so we had to have an extensive safety talk before they allowed us to go below ground. Helmets were to be worn at all times apart from when we were actually shooting, when they were removed and then returned as soon as we had cut. So we made our way down the very long and very steep shaft.

The scenes on that first day were simply us pretending to dig while the actors did their stuff around us.

We were pulled out at one point so that a stunt could happen with a cart. How strange it was, coming back into the light after as so many hours in the shaft!

Tuesday 28th July 2009 – Survivors - Slave Miner

The next morning the second AD came to visit us on the extras bus with good news. As we were so far away from the production's Birmingham base, we were going to get £20 each travel-money per day. This is unheard of outside of London so we were very pleased.

This day we were being shut up in a large metal container and tied to the actors by the neck – lovely! We started off inside the container although no shots were taken inside the box, all that would be in studio a few weeks later. I was pleased to be tied to the actor Paterson Joseph, of whose work I am a fan. After all, he was in Doctor Who, Neverwhere, Hyperdrive and of course, this re-make of Survivors. At the time, he was strongly rumoured to be one of the favourites to play the Eleventh Doctor Who, a role which eventually went to Matt Smith, although those in the know say that Joseph came very close. He was very nice and we talked about the rumours and his chances of being the Doctor. I asked him if it would worry him that if he got the role, it might be that the BBC wanted to be seen as politically correct by casting a black actor in such a high-profile role. He wasn't concerned by any of that. Each episode is so expensive that the BBC would never put being PC ahead of the money that the show generates. He was confident that if he won the role it would be because of his acting abilities alone. I saw his point. Despite this conversation, I did try not to talk too much science fiction, so as to not come across as a complete geek!

Wednesday 29th July 2009 – Survivors - Slave Miner

I don't normally travel to sets with other people as I like to be very early just in case something should go wrong, whereas most other people I know are happy to arrive on time. However on this occasion there happened to be four of us coming from Birmingham where I was staying at my partner's house.

Although I didn't like the idea of not being in control, the money that we would save by car sharing proved to be too good to resist. The plan was for two people to come to my partner's house. I would then drive us to the fourth person's house and he would then drive us to set. In the event, the first person turned up on time, but then we waited and waited. I telephoned the other chap to see where he was.

"I overslept" he said.

"Okay we'll go without you, but you'll have to go and pick up the fourth chap as only you know where he lives"

He didn't like that idea and asked us to wait, promising that he would be there very soon and that we wouldn't be late.

I should have known better, but I agreed anyway and waited. He finally turned up and we went to the other chaps house at full pelt. By the time we arrived we were already cutting it fine and still had another 40 miles to set. We piled into his car and drove off. I just assumed he knew where he was going, and he seemed to be of a similar opinion as he didn't even put his sat-nav on.

I began to get concerned when I noticed the signs indicating that we were getting closer and closer to Shrewsbury, which I'm sure is not that close to Stoke-on-Trent, which is where we should have been heading for. Out came the sat-nav and it quickly became clear that we'd been going the wrong way. We turned the car around only to get caught in a serious traffic jam.

We were now officially late. I phoned the 2nd AD, who told us just to get there as quickly as we could.

We decided to take an alternative route to avoid the traffic, which became the longest cross country detour ever. I was stressing like mad and completely annoying the other chaps. Their attitude was, "Who cares, it's just a TV show", which I completely understood, but at the same time it's just not professional ever to be late.

We finally got there, I found the 2nd AD and couldn't apologise enough. The situation was made far worse by the fact that she was giving us travel money and I felt rotten about the whole thing. Just to add the icing to a very sorry cake, the chap who had been late to my house had only texted another extra on set to get him to hold onto a cooked breakfast for him for when he turned up. This made us all look even more like we just didn't care. It was all very embarrassing.

That day we were finally going to be filming outside. There are not many shows that I have particularly ever wanted to be seen on, but this was definitely one of them. However, being blacked up and put down a mine was one sure way that none of us could be recognised. Then they told us that we were to be lined up and marched off somewhere, all joined together!

"Joined together?" we asked.

"Yes, by the neck, on a wire. Oh, and you'll have potato bags on your head!"

That put an end to any idea of getting seen in this show.

We all got to choose our potato bags. They had been pretty well emptied but they weren't by any means new ones and they really smelt.

From inside the bags we just couldn't make out our surroundings as we were marched along by the neck. The secret was to hold onto the wire to make sure that your neck band didn't come off.

Have I not mentioned the neck band yet? It was made to look like a metal band with a padlock on the front (which was exactly what the hero ones were for the close ups) but they were in fact made of plastic and had a Velcro back for easy access. The wire was placed through the padlock.

Lunch was always fun on this show because we were filthy. Extras (of course) always have to wait for the end of the dinner queue before being allowed to eat, which meant that we could spend ages washing our hands. Even so, no matter how long we spent trying to get clean, we would leave the bus covered in black marks all over the tables after we'd eaten. Extras tend to blame the crew for a mess in the dining bus but on this occasion we couldn't.

After we'd eaten we were back in the mines, so no need for the potato bags and this time we were joined by all the main artists.

Paterson Joseph was being taken off to be hanged. We had to look upset by this, and for once I gave it my all!

As I keep repeating, extras are not actors basically because we cannot act, no matter how many part time evening drama classes some extras like to tell you that they've been to. Nonetheless, I decided that this was my shot. I was at the front with the main artists, facing the camera through the gate.

I thought everything in my life that had ever made me sad (especially when my childhood pet rabbit died) and I managed to upset myself enough to really get into the situation as if it was real. They were real tears on my face as I joined the cries of mercy, pleading with the bad guys not to not kill poor Paterson! I've never tried so hard to throw myself into a scene like that before, (that's not our job, we're just extras after all). The camera was coming right up to the gate as we screamed and cried and it came into our faces. The tears were streaming and I didn't blink just to keep them coming. In the end it was all for nothing, I wasn't even in the frame!

For a moment I had actually forgotten that extras don't need to be able to act, as they're not required to!

Thursday 30th July 2009 – Survivors - Slave Miner

A couple of us were called in early the next day to be told that one of us would have a speaking role. Again, usually I really don't care if I speak or not as it's just a job and I never actually watch any of these shows. But this was Survivors and I wanted it!

The other guy selected is a really nice chap and a friend of mine, but he's had more than his fair share of speaking roles over the years and he's a firm favourite with the Midlands agent, who he's always telling us, looks after him more than most. I wanted this role!

We were both on the bus in costume and the 1st AD came to get us, (very unusual!)

He told us what the role was but made it clear that he didn't know which one of us he wanted to give it to.

We went down the mine and into a whole new area that we hadn't been in before. The 1st explained that one of us would be down at the bottom with Paterson and the other would be at the top collecting the bucket from these guys.

The 1st still hadn't said who was going to do the role and so I guess we both figured we were in the running.

The 1st AD then went to ask if either of us would be happy to climb that far down. My hat goes off to the other extra, as before I knew it, he had said "I'll do it," had pushed past me and started climbing down the ladder!

I had lost out again, but to be fair, the 1st AD said nothing so I guess he wanted the other chap all along.

Because he'd got those lines, it meant that he then got some more later on. It only mattered to me so much because I'm such a science fiction junky

Later in the afternoon we were doing a scene which came just before the first scene that we filmed in the house on our first day - the escape from the mines and the killing of the bad guys.

This was brilliant fun as we got to run around and make lots of noise.

We then had to do a wild track of the same scene, which is a sound recording of background noise to be played behind the actors' dialogue. This was even more fun as we got to scream and shout at each other as if with murderous intent. We could shout at anyone or anything we wanted including crew, other extras and even inanimate objects!

Later on there was a brilliant explosion as they blew up a car. I wasn't on set at the time but I was in direct line of sight to the explosion. I wanted to video it so much from my telephone but I figured that if I got caught I would be sacked and in any case I would see it again on TV.

Tuesday 4th August 2009 –

Britain's Fattest Man – Spectator

I went up to Rochdale for this TV movie, which starred Bobby Ball. It was filmed right outside the Waterloo Road school gates, so I took the opportunity to phone some of the extras inside just to wave at them.

The scene had us watching a giant TV set on which the title character was being weighed as we cheered him on.

Bobby Ball came out to speak to everyone after the shoot and I had a photo taken with him! This is something that I never ask for unless I am absolutely certain that the actor concerned won't mind – which some most certainly do - which explains why this book isn't full of photographs of me with all the famous people whom I have mentioned

It's funny in this job, you regularly see the world's biggest stars, and yet there are only a few of them that you really want to meet – usually the ones whom you've grown up watching.

Wednesday 5th August 2009 – Survivors - Slave Miner

Back in Birmingham we were based at the old ITV studios where many years ago, they used to make all manner of well-known shows, including the infamous long-running soap Crossroads. By now, the studio was awaiting demolition and had very much fallen into disrepair. It was just a big hollow space, even all the sound proofing had been ripped off the walls. It was perfect for Survivors.

It was here where they had built the interior of the container in which I was supposed to be strapped to Paterson.

I sat there all day but seemed to be on the other side of the camera most of the time. I had turned down a six day shoot with dialogue and fighting on another show in order to be here so as not to mess up the continuity, so I wasn't best pleased.

With the studio was in such a state, there were no toilets so we had to use the facilities at a nearby hotel.

It was a lot of fun, turning up at the hotel, looking like a bunch of homeless people, so we decided it was a good time for a photo shoot.

BrightHouse – 2009 – George the Bear

During 2009 my partner and I did another job outside of extra work. When I was first asked to do this, I couldn't believe that I had now reached such a low point in my life that I had gone from being Head of Internal Corporate's for one of the biggest retailers in the country to dressing up as a bear and dancing for the public! The thing was, the job paid very well. I got to work with my partner and we got to go around the country staying in hotels together all on expenses. Plus we were only working 6 hours a day, with twenty minutes on followed by thirty minute breaks.

It was tough but lots of fun. We would dance and dance and then there would be kids clinging to our legs and people wanting their photograph taken with us.

Extra Time

My partner did a Bhangra dance that got so much attention that people would film it and put it on YouTube!

The weird thing was that we were such the centre of attention in the bear outfits and then when we took a break and took the costumes off, we would walk out of the shops and no-one would take the slightest notice of us.

I started doing as much George the Bear work as possible, usually three days a week from Friday to Sunday as BrightHouse were opening new stores all around the country.

This went on for several months and it was nice to have regular money coming in, almost like a real job, but then suddenly without warning it stopped. We tried to find out what had happened but we weren't hired by directly BrightHouse, rather by a DJ who himself was working for the company, so no one could tell us why we weren't being hired any more. So, it was back to just doing extra work.

Meanwhile Producer Dominic Took, for whom I had worked way back on 'No Justice, Just Us', got in touch. He had been trying to put a feature film together for a while and had got Steve Bishop to write a script and brought Tony Jopia on board as director.

Filming was to start in November and he asked me if I'd like to come on board as 1st AD. The film was to be called Deadtime.

I was getting fed up with just doing extra work and really wanted to get back into making stuff! This is what I had left my job at Morrison's for, but realistically I was just too old to go into a TV show and start as a runner, at which I wouldn't be any good in any case, I simply can't keep that big annoying mouth of mine shut!

Working on the pre-production of Deadtime taught me so much. Tony (the director) would talk to me every day about what had gone well and what had not, and particularly about what I had done well or otherwise.

Tuesday 25th August 2009 - Paradox – Agent

This must be one of the most uneventful and unmemorable shows that I've ever been on. I can't remember hardly anything at all about it – just vague memories of walking around some offices in Manchester. This isn't entirely unusual for me, there are even some quite well known shows that I've been on - even I have heard of them, and I've seen the photographic evidence that I was there, and yet I still have no recollection of them whatsoever.

Thursday 27th August 2009 – Crash – Doctor

In this job we tend to work on a lot of shows that no one has heard of, often simply because they are new shows, but you kind of expect to hear of them later on. Well I've still never heard of this one.

It was hospital show filmed in Caerphilly, which we were told, would be a British version of Scrubs.

I was a Doctor for a change and just did the usual Doctor stuff, walking about and then running up to a person who'd collapsed on the floor. That's about as exciting as it got but there were a whole bunch of nice extras on this show, which made it worthwhile.

I got a phone call while I was on this show, asking if I would like to do four days on EastEnders as a member of a jury. If you ever want your own close-up on TV, be on a jury and sit in the front row in the middle. Close-up guaranteed! But being on a jury on a TV show is the most boring job on the planet. Imagine sitting in a court room, listening to the same speeches over and over again as they get new shots. Trying to stay awake is nearly impossible. On the plus side, it was four days' work, so I wasn't going to grumble.

I was also offered the chance to be put forward as a cameraman on a kids' TV show, which would also be four days – the same four days. It would have to be the one or the other, I couldn't do both. "Sorry EastEnders. Yes please the kids' show."

I got a call back later that day to say I had got the kids' show job, but that it was now as a vision mixer, rather than a cameraman - and it was only a one day shoot! I had turned down four days on EastEnders for a one day shoot!

Friday 28th August 2009 - Hustle – Diner

We were booked as diners on Hustle, which by now was filming in Birmingham, having moved out of London (although it still pretends that it's in London).

Another bonus about this job is that sometimes we get to go to places where we wouldn't normally be welcome. That day we were in a very expensive and I imagine very exclusive diners' club in the centre of Birmingham.

The guest actor in this episode was Daniel Mays whom at the time I had never heard of, but who has since become famous for his electrifying performances in Ashes to Ashes, Doctor Who, Treasure Island and almost everything else that has been good on television in recent years. He proved to be very friendly, speaking to everybody. He was, however very loud, but I guess that was just the character he was playing.

The waiter in this episode was played by another friendly young actor, called Adam Fray. He sounded pretty pleased and pleasantly surprised about getting a small acting job even though he had fewer lines than an extra with dialogue usually gets!

Adam was really cool and didn't have any of the "us and them" attitudes that actors sometimes have. Being new to TV he'd not yet learnt how low we extras are on the ladder.

I mention Adam because we have since become great friends and he's a very talented young actor.

Extra Time

I was sitting with my real life partner and two extras who had never done it before. Now, the last thing an extra should ever do is to give advice to other extras, as we're all at the bottom of the pile together, but on this occasion, I broke that rule. These two ladies, along with the rest of us, had been told to mime. Surely, miming is not a difficult concept to grasp, but you wouldn't believe how many people seem to feel that when they mime, they have to over-compensate for the lack of sound coming out of their mouths. Many even confuse miming with whispering. I don't think they understand just how much sound the microphone picks up. You can whisper across the room and it will be picked up by the sound guys. This was very much one of those bad miming occasions.

Background extras sometimes fall into four categories: Firstly there are the whisperers, who come in very close to each other, so as to hear what the other person is saying. This looks very silly as generally people don't get that close whilst chatting.

Then there are the pointers, the over compensating mimers, who have to exaggerate every single movement of their bodies while pretending to talk non-stop with big wide open mouths. Oh, and they have to point!

The Zombies are those extras who are never quite comfortable when a camera is pointed in their direction. They just can't relax. They can be spotted by their strange zombie walk, with eyes forward, arms straight down at their sides, almost as if they are being pulled along on a trolley!

Finally there are the rhubarbs, normal, relaxed, comfortable extras who just mime and respond to other people's mimes, even though neither has any idea what the other is talking about. They move as little and as often as necessary to keep the scene alive but at the same time they don't distract the audience from the main performance.

Well, on his occasion we had two pointers on our table! They were talking non-stop, making it look like they were talking over each other and pointing at everything they could see!

My partner and I just read the menu and ignored them out of shame!

I simply had to point this out politely to them and suggested that it might be an idea if they were to look at each other, so one wasn't talking over the other. Does this make me a bad person?

Thursday 3rd/Friday 4th/Monday 7th September 2009 –

Jinx – Diner

I got three days in Manchester on a kids TV show being made by an independent company at the BBC studios. All I had to do was to sit with my TV daughter, pretending to eat and drink while the action went on around the room.

Everybody was so nice on this show and the days weren't all that long, but apart from that,

I can't actually remember much about this show. Most the other extras were kids with only two of us adults.

Tuesday 8th September 2009 – Hounded – TV Editor

I had been penciled in for a week on this show but ended up doing only one day whilst my partner got the whole week.

Extra Time

We filmed in the BBC Wood Lane centre and were all playing crew on a TV show! My partner was make-up and I was the editor. Others were camera men and producers and the like.

This was a children's show starring the comedian Rufus Hound whose character in the show is a guest on a TV show!

Each episode starts the same way and takes place on the same day, with Rufus getting out of bed, going to the BBC centre and starting on the show. Then a future version of Rufus turns up in the editing suite behind where I am working and sends the present day Rufus into another story, which all ends up with the original day not actually having existed! Understand? It's confusing.

The other extras were used all day in the studio while I sat on my own reading my book until finally after lunch the "real" crew came out into the waiting area and explained my section.

All I had to do was pretend to be editing the show and not even to notice the future Rufus coming in behind me. Nice! I was pleased that I was going to be allowed to play with the real BBC editing suite, as it's a tad bigger than my own. However, I was told in no uncertain terms that I wasn't to touch anything, just to only pretend to press the buttons in front of me.

The scene took about 45 minutes to complete and that was it. I was wrapped.

Would you believe, this was one of the highest paid jobs that I've ever done as an extra?

This scene was classed as "walk-on" or "featured" (more money) which meant I got repeat fees. The scene went on to appear in every single episode of that season, so I got paid for every episode and the repeats. Nice indeed!

I was hoping that we would be asked back for the next season but it wasn't to be.

Thursday 17th September 2009 –

5 Days – Actor double/train passenger/Railway employee

This was filmed on a train up in Derbyshire. It was toward the end of the shoot and as far as I knew, I was going to play a train passenger.

We had breakfast at the station and then boarded the train. I sat in my seat reading a book hoping to simply be able to sit there all day reading and getting paid for it. (Is that called lazy or simply being a keen reader?)

Then costume came along and told me that I was going to be playing a railway employee and later on would have to get out onto the tracks, as someone was supposed to have jumped off a bridge onto the track and been run over. I wondered who that would be.

I got dressed in my orange florescent jacket and hard hat and sat in my train seat until I was called for.

I was in a seat towards the front of the train with only a couple of extras. The others had gone to the back of the train away from the crew. I mention this as I think they had mistaken me for someone else, who must have been elsewhere on the train. Anyway, while I was sitting there a man came along and told me that I was a double for one of the actors.

I said I hadn't been made aware of this but did as I was asked and followed him to the costume team again.

Extra Time

They said I would be playing the train employee later but for now I was to double for the actor who throws himself off the bridge.

Normally I wouldn't think much of this but on this occasion the actor in question was an Asian man dressed as an Asian woman, complete with burka!

It took a surprisingly long time for the burka to be wrapped around my head.

The train had stopped and a makeshift gangplank had been made for us to get off and climb the bank to the bridge where my costume was finalised. I was then placed onto a box to look over the parapet.

The shot was from the train looking up at me, and from the side of the bridge. (You can actually tell it's me even under all that costume by the way I slouch when I walk!)

I didn't have to throw myself off the bridge or even lie on the tracks but I was quickly changed, without ever managing to get a photograph of the outfit, back into my railway employee costume, in which I appeared in the next scene, waving the train on after the accident. Finally I was changed back into my own clothes and became a passenger on the train that I had just stopped by jumping off the bridge and started off again by waving it on! Talk about a busy day. No time for reading.

I got a call to ask if I wanted to go back onto Waterloo Road the next day, as the teacher again, but I turned it down and ended up leaving that agency as that was all they seemed to offer me. Plus I was booked to do EastEnders that day.

Friday 18th September 2009 – EastEnders – Passer-by

I wouldn't normally put a passer-by job in this book as we do so many of them and they're what extras were made for; but I'd not done EastEnders before and I was quite excited to finally walk around the set.

It was a lot smaller than I had expected and after about an hour the excitement wore off and it became just another job.

I did fall asleep outside on a bench while I was waiting to be used, so it was nice to be able to say that this was another famous set that I'd slept on.

Sunday 4th October 2009 – Being Human – Postman

I was surprised to get what could have been a featured role on this show as I'd not done it before. I think I would have liked to have been a vampire but I wasn't complaining at being a postman!

It was really early on a Sunday morning, when the show was still being filmed in Bristol. My scene was supposed to be first but it got swapped until a little later.

I got there, changed into costume and then went to set, which was a real street on which props had put fake post boxes outside all the shops.

While I stood there watching the filming I spotted a face that I knew, but it took a while for me to realise who it was.

He spoke first. "Hello again," he said. As soon as he opened his mouth I knew who he was. It was Bryan Dick whom I'd met at a read through a while back and then again on the set of Lewis.

Bryan told me about all the stuff that he had done since I last saw him, and that he was going onto Ashes to Ashes the following week. I had already asked him to come along as a guest to the Whoovers Doctor Who Group in Derby (following his role in Torchwood), but he had never agreed, so I felt it best not to harass him. I'm sure there's a rule somewhere about harassing actors!

In the scene they filmed first Lenora Crichlow was being kidnapped and dragged into a room after trying to help a guy who was lying injured on the floor... or something. The truth is that I have never seen the show even though I know I would love it. I am waiting for the price of Blu rays to come down! Anyway, after this I was introduced to her and I mentioned that I had enjoyed her in Doctor Who. She seemed really nice.

My scene was right at the start of the episode, so it was padded out a little. All I had to do was deliver some letters and ignore Lenora while she spoke to me.

We did a few takes but it didn't take long until I was wrapped.

Monday 12th – Thursday 15th October 2009 –

Poirot – Policeman

I always love doing the Agatha Christie shows so I was very pleased to be offered several days on Poirot. Even better, the episode (called Halloween Party) was written by Mark Gatiss for whom I have a lot of respect, as he is a brilliant actor/writer and a big Doctor who fan! (I would love to see him taking over the running of Doctor Who one day).

Unfortunately I didn't get to see Mark on the set but as always with these productions, there was an amazing cast, which included Zoë Wannamaker and Julian Rind-Tutt.

According to the script we were a "gaggle" of police even though there were in fact only two of us for the entire episode.

My fellow police officer was an old friend of mine called Ian Harding, with whom I had spent a lot of time on Gulliver's Travels, and struggling to learn that dance.

The location was the garden of a very old house near Windsor, with topiary hedges cut into amazing shapes. Ian and had to start off hiding in the garden. Then when Poirot (played by David Suchet) called out we had to run out of the hedges, chase and arrest Julian Rind-Tutt.

Julian turned out to be a lovely down to earth chap. I think I had seen him on TV as a bad guy so many times, that I didn't expect him to be so nice. It was weird being told to be a little rough with him when we captured and arrested him.

We spent the rest of the week pretty much walking around the gardens and the lakes near the house.

Everybody on this show was fantastic and kind and there was so much respect for David Suchet. Ian and I were even given chairs to sit on while we were waiting around. Being the only two extras, we were a bit surprised, when we were queuing for lunch to be asked if we could hold back for the crew. I know this is the policy but we thought it might be different as there were only two of us.

So we went to the back and waited, while more and more crew kept popping up out of no-where. Just when it seemed we were getting near the front yet more crew would appear and we'd have to wait a bit longer. I am pleased to report that we did manage to eat in the end though.

October 2009 – Deadtime –1ST AD

Pre-production was going ahead at full steam on the low budget feature that we were putting together. Dominic Took had found a brilliant crew.

The Special effects guys were now based in the Wednesbury office and it finally looked like the film really would come together.

Writer Steve Bishop had handed in what we considered the final draft and any more changes would be sent down separately.

Tony Jopia was working hard rehearsing with the actors and we were blocking ready for the shoot in a couple of weeks.

When I left my job at Morrisons, it had been for a reason and this felt like it. I had never been so excited to work so long and hard and for so little money.

I was now having to turn work down, so as to be able to get on with scheduling and planning. The cast were all in place but there were still crew members joining us.

Meanwhile, Matt Hickinbottom had finished writing the pilot for the Fizzogs comedy drama. It went through so many name changes. Matt wanted Black Country in there somewhere. I thought "Thursday" was a good name for some reason but he didn't. However, I like to think that when the name "Black by Day" was finally decided upon, that the "day" part came from my "Thursday" idea.

Matt wanted to shoot this pilot at typically 'super Matt speed' in just two days, slap bang in the middle of when we were shooting "Deadtime"

Prior to this we had filmed a number of short comedy sketches that the 'Fizzogs' girls had written, but Matt wasn't too keen on the comedy sketch idea and so turned the pilot into something with far more solid characters.

Tony Jopia, the director of Deadtime, kindly allowed me to take the time off, so now, having wanting to first (1st?) a show for so long, I was firsting (1st ing?) two shows at the same time!

I was having to turn down so much extra work and typically when you to turn work down, you seem to get offered all the more.

Thursday 22nd -Friday 23rd October 2009 –

Poirot – Policeman

Ian and I were back on Poirot for a 2 day shoot, which was the dénouement of the episode.

We had each been given sides (a breakdown of the shooting days script, usually attached to the call sheet).

I sat at the side of the room to see a pre -camera rehearsal. All the actors were in their respective seats and the First called action just to see the scene for the first time.

David Suchet started talking. Without reference to any sides he did the entire thirteen page dénouement scene, straight off, word perfect. I had never seen anything like it. It was amazing. Even some of the other actors who were in the room, who had very little to say still had a set of sides in their hand as back-up.

All Ian and I had to do was bring the handcuffed Julian Rind-Tutt into the room, then to stand there with him in front of us. It wasn't much, but it was a real honour to see David Suchet at work.

At the end of the second day all the actors wanted to have their photos taken together, so Ian and I were asked to take it in turns to take the photos and to stand in them in our period Police outfits. Of course we wanted to get the pictures on our cameras too, but alas you know the rules on set. No extras can take photos.

Tuesday 27ᵗʰ & Friday 30ᵗʰ October 2009 – EastEnders – CID

I hadn't turned work down completely but I was cutting down. However, when the opportunity came up for a featured role on EastEnders I couldn't say no.

Ian Beale had been hiding a laptop that he'd stolen and we were the CID team that raided his house. I was the one who took the laptop away. It was typical extra work, with the Beale family shouting at me, while all I got to do was to pull my mean face at them without actually say anything. I then had to take the laptop outside (on a different day, as the outside is on the street and the inside is in the studio), to the back of the evidence car. I got a nasty look from Peggy Mitchell (Barbara Windsor), which just made my day. It's great when actors give you a nasty look as part of a scene, rather than just as they pass you on set outside of shooting.

Thursday 5th November 2009 –

A Passionate Woman – Man at a fair

I only mention this show as Billie Piper was in it. I never get fed up with seeing Billie. She's brilliant and really nice.

This was another period show. This time we were at a funfair in Leeds. It was a late call and I had just changed my Northern agent so I didn't want to be late. I gave it plenty of time but still got caught in standstill traffic on the motorway. I contacted the agent to let him know that I might be a tad late and he said just to get there when I can.

As it turned out, I was thirty minutes early, arriving in time for my breakfast at 3.00pm, which is quite normal for night shoots.

This was the first time that I had been allowed to wear my own coat on a period set but I didn't get away with my own trilby as I was told that the rim was too wide for the 1950s.

We got to go on rides and eat toffee apples and candy floss, which was fun the first couple of times. However, I am experienced enough to know never to eat on film, as you usually have to do it over and over again. So, after a few takes, I just started pretending to eat.

On one of the shots there was a shooting. Nobody warned the extras, so that our genuine reactions could be filmed. I jumped out of my skin. It was seriously loud and scared the pants off a few of us, but I guess it was the only way to get some real reaction shots. After all, we extras are not normally known for our acting abilities, are we now?

Saturday 21st November – Monday 7th December 2009 – Deadtime - 1st AD

On Saturday we finally turned over our first shot on Deadtime. Looking back on it, the whole shoot is still pretty much a blur. We fell behind schedule on the first day, (well it was my first time doing this job), and it took a long time to catch up.

We had such a low budget and everyone was working seriously long days and nights. The SFX (Special Effects) team, together with a CGI (Computer Generated Imagery) specialist, did a fantastic job with what they had.

After two days it felt like we had been filming for weeks. I felt so guilty to be going off for two days to make Black By Day.

Monday 23rd November -Tuesday 24th November 2009, Black by Day, 1st AD/Doctor

Matt's script had a character in it that I really wanted to play, but Matt said that the girls already had someone in mind for him, as a consolation, I could play the Doctor instead. This was an unexpected role, which I had no idea how to play.

The doctor was a deaf, blind, pervert, but the role had to be played straight. I had learnt my lines but it seemed an idea to get into costume at the start of the day, as there would be no time to change later, due to the tight schedule, which relied drastically on the light. Due to the time of year, all the daytime shots had to be completed before 4.00pm.

We were so lucky that the girls had done an amazing job and managed to secure the Black Country museum for us to film in, at no cost.

Unlike on Deadtime, this was the smallest crew you could imagine. Matt was DoP (director of photography), gaffer (lighting), cameraman and director. My partner took it in turns with Matt's dad as boom operator. A friend was grips and I was 1st/2nd and 3rd AD. That was the entire crew.

Because the girls had been pointed in my direction to start with and I'd introduced them to Matt, we all shared executive producer roles and owned the concept of the entire show between the five of us.

We all took it in turns to make the coffees and do whatever fetching and carrying was needed and anybody who had a free moment would help someone else. It was a real team effort and it totally paid off as we managed to shoot the entire 25 minute pilot in two fifteen hour days! It was the longest two days ever but we all really enjoyed it and everybody was amazing. It was fun to do and turned out to be fun to watch. We even had a première so that people could come and give their honest opinions about it.

We weren't sure if we were just going to be making just this one episode or trying to shoot a complete six part series. With minimal budget and everyone working for free, this would be hard.

The idea was to use this pilot rather than just a script in order to sell the idea to the TV market, should anyone out there be listening.

After Matt had edited it, put a soundtrack on it and graded it, I spend hours on the internet every night, trying to find the names and contact details of every TV channel commissioning editor, and sending them copies, in the vain hope that someone would actually watch it.

Anyway, I've got a bit ahead of myself. The next day I was back on the set of Deadtime, and within moments it was as if I had never been away.

We had some amazing special guests on Deadtime, all of whom came in and worked for us for free.

Terry Christian was one such guest. I didn't expect much from him, as I had always known him more for his presenting work, rather than as an actor, but he was brilliant. He had seven pages of dialogue and he knew every word. Dominic had also somehow secured the services of Joe Egan who had worked on the Robert Downey Jnr. Sherlock Holmes movie as Big Joe. Leslie Grantham famous as Dirty Den in EastEnders did a day for us as did Ian Hill, bassist with the famous rock band Judas Priest. As it happened, there was a mention of the band in the script. It turned out that one of our runners was Ian Hill's step-son, Dominic asked him nicely and in he came.

This was my first time as a 1st AD on a feature length project so please excuse the fact we got behind schedule. We tried to catch up but it proved impossible without cutting down on shots.

We had to find another way of getting back on track, so Tony Jopia said we would have to have a second unit that could work at the same time as the main unit, at the next location on smaller scenes with any available actors.

So, a second unit was put together and Tony asked me to direct it. Apart from corporate's I'd never directed drama before and I tried everything to get out of it, but in the end here I was, being given everything that I ever wanted on a platter. My own film crew, actors and a location to go and film stuff! Even so, it took a full day for Tony to persuade me that I could do it. Tony taught me so much on this shoot including that I should never let my insecurities show in front of the team, something that you might think I would already know, after so many years running teams at Safeway, but I guess I forgot.

So, off I went to form my own little second unit. We were a much smaller team and were only allowed equipment that wasn't currently being used by the first unit!

Over the next few days we filmed more and more. Some of it was in a freezing old house. It actually snowed on some of the days and there was no heating, but I couldn't complain. I was wrapped up while the poor actors were wearing next to nothing.

The shoot took so much out of all of us but we pulled together as a team and I know we couldn't have tried any harder. It has given me a whole new look on low budget films. I won't just switch them off now if I don't like them, but will look further into how such films have been made with so little money and time.

I had a little story idea, which I mentioned it to Tony Jopia and Steve Bishop (the writer). I thought it might be an idea to have a character in the initial music industry meeting at the start of the film, who just sits there without saying a word. Then at the end of the conversation, he just looks at the music manager and does a slit throat sign, as if to say 'cut the band' but which the audience might think means '*kill* the band', (a bit like the notorious Cigarette-Smoking Man in The X-Files).

Extra Time

They liked this idea so I'm still a little baffled by how the character became an over the top foppish PA for Terry Christian's character, and how I ended up getting the role! I was pleased though to make it into the film.

The film has since been bought by a distributor and is out on DVD from 4DigitalMedia in the UK

So, that's about it really - my life as an extra; eleven years-worth of stories and gossip from various TV and film sets around the country, from the point of view of an extra, the lowest of the low. The film is still out there somewhere, so do feel free to find it, watch it and let us know what you think of it.

As I said at the beginning, if at any point in this book I have come across as in any way negative then please don't believe it for a moment. I love being an extra. In fact, perhaps I love it a little bit too much and I wonder sometimes if that's why I've not gone back into training and video production.

What could be more fun than travelling the country to see so many TV shows and movies being made; seeing my favourite directors and actors and dressing up in so many outfits, pretending to be someone else for the day! What's not to like. But it isn't a career and it is a job that is so very little regarded within the industry. I'm not sure why an out-of-work actor would get more respect for doing a job in a fast food shop, than they would if they got on-set experience as an extra, but that is certainly true.

Sometimes the job costs more in fuel and hotel bills than I actually earn, by the time the agent has had their cut and VAT and National Insurance has been taken out. Then the accountant wants to give some more away in tax at the end of the year too!

As with any book of this sort, I have had to cut out quite a lot. For a start, I haven't said anything at all about my life and career since. There are many stories that remain to be told another time and quite a lot that for reasons of discretion can never be told – such as the time when the star of… (No, I'd better not); then there was the time that I happened to overhear the two married stars of… (No, not that one either). The trouble is that I might be working with these people next week. We extras do have to learn early on to keep our mouths shut – that is if we want to keep on working.

So what about the future? Well, I'd like to go on to direct my own film, a nice low budget horror or sci-fi, so if you have any good ideas or a script, or some thoughts on how to raise the necessary money, then feel free to throw your ideas my way, and we'll get started. In the meantime, my accidental job as a film and TV extra goes on. Every day is different and every job brings new experiences and new stories to tell. I do sometimes hanker after a more settled life – perhaps even a regular 'nine to five' job, but in the end I'm still enjoying what I do, working alongside some of the best-known stars in the country on some of the biggest shows. I am often asked if I would recommend my job to other people who want to get into the film and television industry. Well, certainly not for anyone who wants to become an actor – being stigmatised as an extra is enough to kill off any budding acting career. Being an extra has never really paid enough to be a proper full-time career, but if someone fancies doing it as a side-line, working with their heroes and seeing at close quarters how their favourite shows are made, then why not. Perhaps I'll see you on set one day. Then again, why am I saying that? There are only so many jobs to go around and I need the work.

John R Walker, September 2012

John R. Walker

Dr Who – New Earth (2005)/ Auton 2 Cast and Extras (1998)

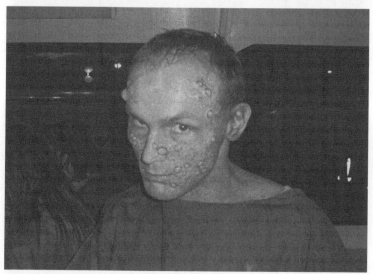

Life on Mars (2005)

AA Advert (2005) above, Heartbeat (2006) Below

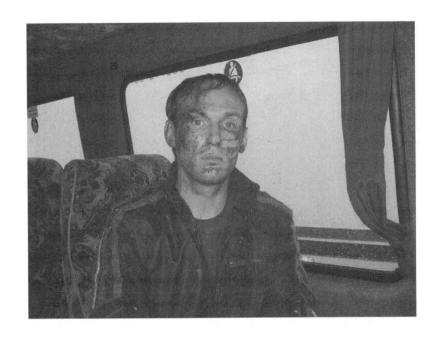

Torchwood (2006) above, Enchantment (2006) Below

John R. Walker

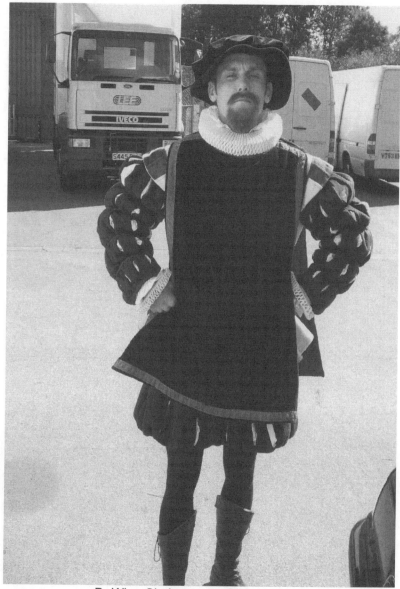

Dr Who; Shakespeare Code

Shameless (2007) above, Torchwood as Cpt John (2007)

Casualty (2008) as young ones above, Sherlock Holmes Movie (2008)
Below

Extra Time

Day of the Triffids (2009)   Being Human (2009) Deadtime (2009) cast

Extra Time

4345758R00164

Printed in Great Britain
by Amazon.co.uk, Ltd.,
Marston Gate.